I0415900

Advisory Circular

U.S. Department of Transportation

Federal Aviation Administration

Subject: GUIDE SPECIFICATION FOR WATER/FOAM AIRCRAFT RESCUE AND FIRE FIGHTING VEHICLES	Date: 2/18/02	AC No: 150/5220-10C
	Initiated by: AAS-100	Change:

1. PURPOSE. This advisory circular (AC) contains performance standards, specifications, and recommendations for the design, construction, and testing of a family of aircraft rescue and fire fighting (ARFF) vehicles.

2. CANCELLATION. AC 150/5220-10B, Guide Specification for Water/Foam Aircraft Rescue and Fire Fighting Vehicles, dated October 20, 1997, is canceled.

3. APPLICATION. The Federal Aviation Administration (FAA) recommends the use of the guidance in this publication for the preparation of ARFF vehicle specifications. For airport projects receiving Federal grant-in-aid assistance, the use of these standards is mandatory. At certificated airports, the use of equipment meeting these standards satisfies the requirements of Title 14 Code of Federal Regulations (CFR) Part 139, Certification and Operations, Land Airports Serving Certain Air Carriers, Subpart D-Operations, Subparagraph 139.317, "Aircraft Rescue and Fire Fighting: Equipment and Agents." Features or design details not listed as required or optional in this document are not considered necessary unless a justification acceptable to the FAA is provided.

DAVID L. BENNETT
Director, Office of Airport Safety and Standards

1

CONTENTS

TABLES

FIGURES

CHAPTER 1. INTRODUCTION.

Section 1. General Characteristics.

1. DEFINITIONS. Terms with meanings unique or specifically related to aircraft rescue and fire fighting (ARFF) vehicle design, construction, and performance requirements are contained in Appendix 1.

2. EXPECTED USE. This guide specification covers two classes of all-wheel drive, diesel-powered ARFF vehicles having a mechanical water/foam system designed for extinguishing flammable and combustible liquid fuel fires. The dry chemical and Clean Agent, or approved equivalent complementary agent systems described in Chapter 3, are acceptable optional additions to the basic vehicle when dictated by local operational needs. However, the primary function of the vehicles described in this guide specification is to provide an optimum level of ARFF suppression capability for the lowest practical cost. These vehicles may also be suitable for other fire protection assignments at the airport. Vehicles complying with this basic specification meet the ARFF vehicle requirements of 14 CFR Part 139.

3. VEHICLE CLASS. The vehicle payload consists principally of the minimum usable (rated capacity) quantities of water shown in Table 1 and sufficient foam concentrate to mix at the appropriate concentration with twice that water quantity.

4. RESERVED.

Table 1. Minimum Usable Water (Rated Capacity).

Class	Gallons	Liters
1	1,500	5,685
2	3,000 and over	11,370 and over

Section 2. Ergonomics.

5. CREW SPACE.

a. All crew space shall be restricted to the interior of a fully enclosed cab with approved, 3-point restraints as minimum seat belts or shoulder harness system.

b. Where practicable, instruments shall be used in preference to warning lights. If warning lights are used, a means to readily test the condition of all warning light bulbs shall be provided.

c. Instruments and warning lights shall be displayed so that they will be useful, convenient, and visible to the driver.

d. The instrument panel(s) shall either be easily removable as units or hinged for back access. Quick disconnect fittings shall be used for all electrical connections to the instrument panel. All instruments, except liquid filled gauges, shall be illuminated. Labels for control and instruments should be backlit or illuminated.

e. All rotating or reciprocating parts, all parts with operating temperatures above 120° F (49° C), or that are electrically energized or are of such a nature or so located as to be a hazard to the safety of operating and maintenance personnel during their normal duties, shall be insulated, enclosed, or guarded as appropriate for the specific hazard and its location.

f. All space that is occupied or from which work is performed during operations, servicing, and maintenance of the vehicles shall be free from hazardous protrusions, sharp edges, cracks, or other elements that might reasonably be expected to cause injury to personnel.

6. RIDE QUALITY.

a. The design objective for the vehicle ride quality shall be to permit safe operation over rough roads and adverse terrain found at the airport of intended service at speeds of at least 35 mph (56 km/h) without causing injury to the operating personnel (wearing seat belts), loss of vehicle control, or damage to the vehicle.

b. The design objective for all vehicle and fire extinguishing system controls shall be to permit driving and fire fighting operations that do not require effort by operating personnel in excess of the limits specified in the current version of MIL-STD-1472, Human Engineering Design Criteria for Military Systems, Equipment and Facilities.

7. CONTROLS.

a. All the controls necessary for the full operation of the vehicle and for activating the fire fighting system shall be within reach of the driver. Controls for the fire extinguishing system(s) shall also be within easy reach of a second crew station or duplicated for that crew station. All cab-mounted controls shall be identified by function and/or limitation with permanent backlit labels.

b. Fire fighting equipment and controls located on the vehicle exterior shall be placed between 24 inches (61 cm) and 72 inches (183 cm) above the ground, catwalks, or deck plates, as applicable.

c. All controls located on the exterior of the vehicle shall be labeled with an illuminated permanent label identifying function and/or limitation.

8. SAFETY FEATURES.

a. A warning siren/device shall be provided, and it shall—

(1) Be a multitone, multivolume state-of-the-art device commonly used in the industry on emergency vehicles. The control(s) shall be accessible to both the driver and a second crew member.

(2) Produce a minimum sound of 95 dB(A) at 100 feet (30 m) directly in front of the vehicle and 90 dB(A) at 100 feet (30 m) and 45 degrees left and right of front center.

(3) Have a speaker mounted as far forward and low as possible and be protected from drippings from the turret and water splashed up by the tires.

b. A horn shall be provided and mounted in accordance with National Fire Protection Association (NFPA) 1901 so as to achieve optimum sound projection to the front of the vehicle. A control button or horn ring shall be located at the steering wheel.

c. A "vehicle backing" warning device, audible up to 25 feet (7.6 m) behind the vehicle, shall be provided. Shifting the transmission into reverse shall activate this device. The volume of the warning device shall be self-adjusting based upon ambient noise.

Section 3. Design Criteria.

9. PERFORMANCE. The design objective for the vehicle and the fire extinguishing system shall be performance in accordance with Chapter 2, Section 7, Automotive Performance. Performance for the fire extinguishing system shall be in accordance with Chapter 3, Section 7, Agent System Performance. Manufacturers shall be required to identify their loaded apparatus's center of gravity as well as the safe operating envelope of the loaded vehicle to include side slope maneuverability and high-speed cornering. Manufacturers shall provide a data plate that contains all the information, at a minimum, presented in Figure 1-4.5 of NFPA 414, Standard for Aircraft Rescue and Fire-Fighting Vehicles, current edition. This data plate shall be installed in the cab of the vehicle and visible to the operator.

10. FLEXIBILITY. The design objective for the vehicle frame, suspension, and mounting of major components shall be to provide the capability for diagonally opposite wheel motion up to 14 inches (36 cm) above the ground without raising the remaining wheels from the ground or causing interference or parts failure.

11. MAINTAINABILITY. The vehicle design shall be such that it—

a. Uses the fewest number of different parts consistent with the specified performance.

b. Permits maintenance with commercially available, general purpose mechanic tools and equipment (metric sizes are permitted if required tools are "standard" and "commercially available" to the extent possible). The vehicle manufacturer shall provide and document in the maintenance manual introduction any special or nonstandard tools required and any unique test equipment required to perform operator/owner maintenance and service.

c. Limits the number of tools and the variety of spare parts required for maintenance by such design practices as reducing the variety of bolt sizes, light bulb sizes, wire gauges, tubing, and pipe sizes as consistent with safety and performance requirements.

d. Uses disconnect plugs, receptacles, junction boxes, bus bars, multiple-line connectors in the electrical systems, and readily detachable fittings in hydraulic and pneumatic systems, as applicable. All disconnect points shall be clearly labeled. All hydraulic and pneumatic lines and electrical wires shall be color-, function-, or number-coded.

e. Includes pilots, guides, slides, carriages, or other features where such provisions can add to the ease of removal and installation or attachment of components.

f. Uses a fastener system that is easily disassembled and reassembled for all cabinets and body-work that must be removed for access for maintenance and removal of components for repair or replacement. Uses fasteners—not limited to brackets, nuts, bolts, washers, screws, and rivets—of stainless steel or other materials resistant to corrosion.

g. Locates drains, filler plugs, grease fittings, hydraulic line-bleeders, and checkpoints so that they are readily accessible and do not require special tools for proper servicing.

h. Ensures that the installation of each major subsystem or critical part can only be in its proper operating position.

i. Provides accessible connections, where needed, to attach troubleshooting, analytical, and diagnostic equipment to appropriate vehicle subsystems.

j. Operates with standard commercial lubricants. Grease and oil seals shall be of a design and located to provide accessibility for inspection, servicing, and replacement. Access to lubrication points shall be provided by means of an easy opening door or hinged panel. Lubrication fittings shall be located in accessible, protected positions. Parts or assemblies that are not readily accessible for direct lubrication, or are likely to be overlooked because of inaccessibility, shall have extended fittings. A safety chain shall attach filler caps to lubrication fill points where practical.

k. Includes, as optional, the installation of continuous duty cycle lubrication systems for suspension lubrication points and other mechanical

equipment joints to increase the duty cycle of components and extend the useful life of the vehicle.

12. COMPONENT PROTECTION.

a. All oil, hydraulic, air, water, foam concentrate, and electrical system conduits, tubing, and hoses shall be located in protected positions. They shall be secured to the frame or body structure and, except where a through-frame connector is necessary, shall be fitted with protective looms or grommets at each point where they pass through panels or structural members.

b. All radiator grills, louvers, lamps, tie rods, drive shafts, piping, and other vulnerable components shall be protected by component location or by guards adequate to prevent damage from brush, stones, logs, etc. likely to be encountered by the vehicle during off-road performance.

13. PAINTING, MARKING, AND LIGHTING. Vehicles shall be painted and marked in accordance with the standards of AC 150/5210-5B, Painting, Marking, and Lighting of Vehicles Used on an Airport.

14. INSULATION, WATERPROOFING, AIR CONDITIONING, AND WINTERIZATION.

a. Insulation shall be fire and water resistant and of a type that will not pack or settle. Provision shall be made to allow the drainage of water from between the walls by gravity flow. The average heat loss shall not exceed 0.24 BTU/ft^2 (0.76 W/m²) per degree Fahrenheit per hour. All insulation that could be exposed to abrasion or damage from equipment storage or operator activities shall be provided with a protective covering. All insulation that will be located on the exterior of the vehicle shall be protected from damage or exposure by a permanent cover to be constructed to match the vehicle exterior.

b. All components shall be designed, installed, and/or protected so that their normal function will not be impaired by heavy rains, road splash, formation of condensation, or the spillage of extinguishing agents from nozzles and fittings, recharging operations, or leaks in the piping system.

c. The normal temperature design criteria shall be for vehicle use in a temperature range of 32° F (0° C) to 115° F (43.5° C).

d. If, in the judgment of the purchaser, the operational practices of the ARFF service at a specific airport warrant the use of air conditioning, a system that meets current automotive/truck and environmental protection standards for vehicle air conditioning may be specified by the purchaser. The use of the air conditioning shall not change the acceptable pass/fail criteria for any of the performance tests of the vehicle or the fire fighting system.

e. If, in the judgment of the purchaser, the climatic conditions combined with the normal operational procedures at a specific airport warrant the use of special freeze protection, a winterization system that meets the requirements of Paragraph 50 may be specified by the purchaser.

15. MATERIALS.

a. Materials not specifically covered by this specification or applicable referenced specifications or standards shall be of the best quality currently used in commercial practice for ARFF vehicle fabrication.

b. Dissimilar metals shall not be in contact with each other. Metal plating or metal spraying of dissimilar base metals to provide electromotively compatible abutting surfaces is acceptable. The use of dissimilar metals separated by suitable insulating material is permitted, except in systems where bridging

of insulation materials by an electrically conductive fluid can occur.

c. Materials that deteriorate when exposed to sunlight, weather, or operational conditions normally encountered during service shall not be used or shall have a means of protection against such deterioration that will not prevent compliance with performance requirements.

d. Protective coatings that chip, crack, or scale with age or extremes of climatic conditions or on exposure to heat shall not be used.

e. The use of proven, nonmetallic materials in lieu of metal is permitted if that use contributes to reduced weight, lower cost, or less maintenance and there is no degradation in performance or increase in long-term operations and maintenance costs.

16. THROUGH 19. RESERVED.

CHAPTER 2. AUTOMOTIVE SYSTEM.

Section 1. Frame.

20. BALANCE AND CLEARANCES.

a. The weight shall be distributed as equally as practical over the axles and tires of the fully laden vehicle.

(1) The difference in tire load between tires on any axle shall not exceed 5 percent of the average tire load for that axle.

(2) The difference in load between axles shall not exceed 10 percent of the load on the heaviest axle.

(3) The front axle shall not be the most heavily loaded axle.

EXCEPTION: The front axle may be the most heavily loaded axle in those cases where options specified by the purchaser cannot be practically engineered to conform to this requirement. However, if the front axle is the most heavily loaded, the weight difference between it and any other axle shall not exceed 5 percent. In addition, none of the component ratings shall be exceeded to accommodate this deviation in the balance/weight distribution AND all other performance requirements of this specification shall be met.

(4) Under no circumstances shall axle and tire manufacturer's ratings be exceeded in an effort to comply with any of the above.

b. The fully loaded vehicle shall be able to meet the side slope stability standards of Table 2, Performance Parameter 2.

c. See Table 2, Performance Parameters 4 through 8, for standard clearances.

21. DIMENSIONS.

a. The overall height, length, and width of the vehicle shall be the smallest dimensions consistent with the rated payload for its class and the operational performance requirements of the vehicle.

b. Although payload and operational performance are of primary importance, cost-effectiveness and local functional consideration (e.g., existing door, bridge, and tunnel clearances) may dictate that one or more specific dimensional requirements be specified by the purchaser.

22. LOAD RATING.

a. The functional load rating of the frame shall equal or exceed the actual gross vehicle weight (GVW). The GVW includes complete chassis; cab with attachments, accessories, and equipment; the body with rated agent payload, including a full complement of crew, fuel, lubricant, coolant, firefighter protective clothing, equipment, and breathing apparatus in appropriate numbers; and fire fighting handtools and appliances.

b. The frame shall not be altered during installation of the fire protection package in any way that will reduce its load rating.

Section 2. Body Components.

23. COACH WORK. Parts shall be fabricated from materials that will provide the lightest weight consistent with the needs for strength, as well as heat and corrosion resistance. Safety of the crew shall be a primary consideration in coach work, especially the protection of occupants during a roll over.

24. COMPARTMENTS. The compartments shall be of weather-tight construction and equipped with closures. Closures shall have positive holding mechanisms in both open and closed positions and may be of track/roll or hinge/swing type.

All compartments shall—

a. Be provided with weather proof lights that are switched to automatically light when compartment doors are opened and the vehicle master switch is in the "on" position.

b. Include vent(s) with a total of at least 10 squares inches (64.5 cm²) of ventilation.

c. Have a drain to allow collected water to run out under the vehicle.

d. Be equipped with an indicator light in the cab or on the instrument panel and an audible signal to advise the operator when a compartment door is open.

e. All compartments shall contain a highly visible, permanently affixed label clearly stating the maximum weight that can be placed therein based upon tilt table certification testing.

25. HANDRAILS. Handrails or a guardrail shall be provided for personnel safety at all steps, walkways, and elevated workstations, including along the vehicle tank top or tank-top fill area. The rail material shall be heat and corrosion-resistant or provided with a low-maintenance, durable, and sunlight-, weather-, heat-, and corrosion-resistant finish. The finish should be slip resistant.

26. RUNNING BOARDS, STEPS, WALKWAYS, AND TOWING DEVICES.

a. Running boards, step surfaces, ladder rungs, walkways, and catwalks shall have antiskid treads, deck plates, handrails, and guards, as applicable.

(1) The height between steps shall be less than 20 inches (50 cm).

(2) The lower steps shall be less than 24 inches (60 cm) from the ground. The lowermost

steps may extend below the angle of approach or departure or ground clearance limits if they are designed to swing clear.

(3) The tread of the bottom steps shall be at least 8 inches (20 cm) in width and succeeding steps at least 16 inches (40 cm) in width.

(4) The full width of all steps shall have at least 6 inches (15 cm) of unobstructed toe room or depth when measured from and perpendicular to the front edge of the weight-bearing surface of the step.

b. Catwalks and deck plates that provide access to equipment mounted on the vehicle shall withstand the loads imposed by personnel while performing normal service and operational functions.

c. Two towing hooks/eyes with shackles shall be attached directly to the frame rails at the front and rear of the vehicle. The purchaser may request a pintle hook having a 30,000-pound capacity rating be attached to the rear frame cross member of the vehicle if its presence will not interfere with other components necessary for the required performance. The towing devices may be allowed to intrude into the 30-degree approach angle in order to provide ease of connection if needed.

Section 3. Cab and Accessories.

27. CONTROLS. Unless otherwise noted, the following cab-mounted controls shall be provided as applicable for the safe and efficient operation of the vehicle:

Accelerator Pedal
Agent Flow Control
Air Conditioner Controls, if specified
Brake Pedal
Complementary Agent/System Activation, if specified
Differential Lock Control
Headlight Dimmer Control
Heated Mirror Control, if specified
Dome Light Switch Manual/Door Activated, with white/red or green light selector switch as specified
Engine Shutdown Switch
Foam Concentrate Reservoir Control Valve
Headlight Switch
Heater/Defroster Controls
Horn Control

Ignition Switch
Master Electrical Disconnect Switch
Panel Lights Switch with Dimmer
Parking Brake Control
Power Adjustable Mirror Control
Siren Switch with Microphone
Switch(es) for Exterior Lights, as specified in Paragraph 39
Switch(es) for Emergency Beacon(s)/ Strobe(s)
Switch(es) for Non-Emergency Amber (Yellow) Beacon(s)/Strobe(s), if specified
Starter Switch
Tilt/Telescoping Steering Wheel Column
Transmission Range Selector
Turret Control
Water Flow Control Valve
Windshield Deluge System Control, if specified
Windshield Wiper and Washer Controls

28. CREW SPACE AND DOORS.

  a. The cab shall—

  (1) Have seats for a driver and at least one additional crewmember. The purchaser may specify additional crew positions if they have a local operational requirement.

  (2) Have space for the instruments, radios, controls, and the safety equipment required for the number of firefighters intended to occupy the cab, without hindering crew operations.

  (3) Have door(s) that open to at least a 90-degree angle and are located on each side of the cab with appropriate steps and hand grabs. The location of vehicle components or mounted fire fighting equipment shall not obstruct the cab entrances/exits or obstruct visibility through the windshield or driver view of mirror.

  (4) Be constructed and/or so mounted on the vehicle frame so as to meet the provisions of Paragraph 10.

  (5) Be constructed to prevent cab collapse in the event of a vehicle rollover.

  (6) Be weathertight and fully insulated in accordance with the provisions of Paragraph 14.

  b. The cab roof shall have gutters of sufficient size to prevent foam and water from dripping on the windshield and side windows during turret operation. All cab fresh air vents/intakes shall be baffled and drained in such a way that wind-driven rainwater and/or water-foam solution sprayed on the vehicle cannot flow into the crew compartment through the air intakes. Fresh air intakes need to be placed and sealed so as to minimize ground fire and/or smoke from a fire environment from entering into the crew space.

  c. All glass shall be a laminated or tempered, tinted safety type that meets applicable Federal standards and shall be free of imperfections that affect visibility.

  d. The design and arrangement of the cab and components shall optimize visibility for a seated driver having an eye height of 31.75 inches (80 cm).

  (1) The lateral field of vision shall be at least 90 degrees left and right of center.

  (2) The ground must be visible to the driver at a point at least 15 feet (4.5 m) and beyond from the vehicle through the left two-thirds of the included angle of vision and 30 feet (9 m) from the vehicle through the right third of the included angle.

  EXCEPTION: Proportional modification of the horizontal visibility range is acceptable for other than a left-mounted driver seat.

  (3) The angle of visibility above the horizontal for the seated driver looking through the front cab windows shall be at least 5 degrees. For vehicles equipped with high-reach, extendible turrets, the angle of visibility above the horizon shall extend to a point 30 feet (9 m) above ground level at a distance of 15 feet (4.5 m) in front of the vehicle.

  (4) Restriction of the horizontal angle of vision by window frames, corner and doorposts, etc. shall not exceed 7 degrees per obstruction.

  (5) Forward vision for the driver, looking through the windshield between the forward corner posts of the cab, shall be unobstructed.

  EXCEPTION: A center post is acceptable if the width is under 2 inches (50 mm) and there are no blind areas at a distance of 40 feet (12 m) from the vehicle when viewed by the driver using both eyes and sitting in a normal operating position.

  e. Cab interior noise level at the driver's ear position (eye height in Paragraph (d) above) shall not exceed 85 dB(A) as specified in Paragraph 2-11.3 of NFPA 414.

  f. An adjustable rearview mirror with a flat glass area of at least 60 square inches (385 cm^2) on each side of the vehicle shall be included. In addition to each flat mirror, a wide-angle convex mirror of at least 7 square inches (45 cm^2) shall be provided. Power adjustable mirrors are required, with their controls installed within easy reach of the driver. Heated mirrors may be specified by the purchaser.

  g. At least one front overhead or two side-mounted (one on each side of the windshield) mirror(s) shall be provided to permit the vehicle operator a clear view of the area in front of the vehicle that is not within the operator's direct view.

  h. The purchaser may specify a monitoring and data acquisition system (MADAS) for the collection of various performance measurements to monitor, as a minimum, the following:

(1) Vehicle speed

(2) Vehicle heading

(3) Lateral acceleration

(4) Vertical acceleration

(5) Longitudinal acceleration and deceleration

(6) Engine rpm

(7) Throttle position

(8) Steering input

(9) Vehicle braking input (pedal position and brake pressure)

(10) Date, time, and location for all data collected

The MADAS shall be capable of scoring the measurements and the time intervals, starting at least 120 seconds before and ending at least 15 seconds after any serious incident. The system shall be designed so that the data being recorded will not be lost or overwritten immediately after the incident due to the use of an emergency shutoff or a master electrical disconnect switch.

i. A lateral stability indicator that is preset by manufacturer for sensitivity and that provides both visual and audio signals and warnings to the driver shall be provided.

29. EQUIPMENT. The following shall be provided as applicable:

Air Conditioner, if specified

Backup monitor, if specified

Cab Dome Light, Red/White

Crew Seats(s), with approved three-point seat belts

Driver's Seat, up and down and fore and aft adjustable, bucket-type with approved three-point seatbelt

FLIR Camera, with a 10-inch minimum monitor

Heater/Defroster, with 200 BTU output per cubic foot of cab space, blower capacity equal to one cab volume per minute, fresh air intake, and ducts to windshield

Navigation and/or Tracking subsystems of a Driver's Enhanced Vision System (DEVS), if specified

Siren/Audible Emergency Warning Device

Sun Visors, two or more

Windshield Deluge System, if specified

Windshield Washers, two or more with a large capacity reservoir

Windshield Wipers, two or more with delayed and multispeed capability

30. INSTRUMENTS AND WARNING LIGHTS. The following instruments and warning lights shall be provided in the cab as applicable:

Air Pressure (brake and other air-driven accessories)

Complementary Agent Tank–Charged Light, if applicable

Compartment Door Indicator

Differential Lock Indicator

Beacon/Strobe Indicator (s)

Engine Coolant Temperature

Engine Oil Pressure

Engine Tachometer(s)

Foam Agent Tank Level Indicator, with test switch

Foam Pump Pressure Indicator, if applicable

Fuel Level

Headlight Beam Indicator

High-reach Turret Deployed Indicator, if a high-reach turret is specified

Illuminated Side/Slope Inclinometer

Lateral Stability Indicator with visual and audible alarm

Low Air Pressure Warning

Low Oil Pressure/High Water Temperature Audible/Visual Alarm

Low Engine Coolant Audible/Visual Alarm

Speedometer/Odometer

Voltmeter, expanded scale

Water Pump Pressure

Water Tank Level Indicator, with test switch

Section 4. Driveline and Controls.

31. AXLES.

a. The axles shall be rated and certified as required by Paragraphs 100.a.(1) and 103.a as being suited for the intended use. The axle manufacturer's approved rating shall not be raised by the vehicle manufacturer to conform to the requirements of this specification.

b. Front and rear axles shall have adequate capacity to carry the fully loaded vehicle under all intended operating conditions. The maximum variation in axle tread shall not exceed 20 percent of the tire(s) sectional width at rated load.

c. Tractive power at each wheel shall be achieved by use of torque proportioning differentials or other suitable automatic devices that will ensure that each wheel of the vehicle is driven independently of the other wheels.

d. Front axles shall be equipped with steering drive ends designed to eliminate fluctuations in angular velocity of the wheels when cramped either left or right at all normal operating speeds.

32. BRAKE SYSTEM. A brake system shall be provided that has been tested and certified in accordance with the applicable requirements of Paragraphs 104, 105, and 106. The system shall include an all-wheel, split-circuit, power-assisted service brake; a modulatable emergency brake; and a parking brake.

a. Air supply. Vehicles supplied with air brakes shall have—

(1) A compressor that shall—

(a) Be engine driven.

(b) Have capacity sufficient to increase air pressure in the supply and service reservoirs from 85 to 100 psi (552 to 690 kPa) when the engine is operating at the vehicle manufacturer's maximum recommended revolutions per minute, in 25 seconds or less.

(c) Have the capacity for buildup of tank pressure from 5 psi (35 kPa) to the pressure required to release the spring brakes within 12 seconds.

(d) Have an automatic air drying system immediately downstream from the compressor.

(2) A service air reservoir that shall—

(a) Have a volume at least 12 times the total combined brake chamber volume at full stroke. If the reservoir volume, inclusive of supply lines and air dryer volumes, is greater than the minimum required, proportionately longer buildup time is acceptable using the following formula:

$$\text{Maximum Time (sec)} = \frac{\text{Actual reservoir capacity x 25}}{\text{Required reservoir capacity}}$$

and

(b) Have drains and safety valves, as necessary for safe and efficient operation. Drains shall be located at the lowest point of the vehicle and be accessible from the side(s) of the vehicle.

(3) When an auxiliary 110/220 VAC air compressor is specified by the purchaser, the shoreline electrical connection, which will release automatically (auto-eject) without damage to the vehicle upon starting the vehicle, shall be supplied.

(4) An automatic release (auto-eject) air connection for the charging of air tanks from an external air source.

(5) Visual and audible low air pressure warning devices. The low-pressure warning device shall be visible and audible from inside the cab.

b. Emergency Brake.

(1) The emergency brake shall be operable by the driver and shall be capable of modulation through the use of the service brake control.

(2) The emergency brake shall be capable of meeting the emergency brake stopping distance standard of Table 2, Performance Parameter 11, with the failure of only a single part in the service brake system other than failure of a common valve, manifold, brake fluid housing, or a break chamber housing.

c. Parking Brake. The parking brake shall be operable by the driver and shall meet the parking brake holding performance standard of Table 2, Performance Parameter 12.

d. Service Brake. A service brake powered by air, hydraulic, or air over hydraulic at the manufacturer's option, which meets the applicable performance standards of Table 2, shall be acceptable.

(1) A chamber shall be provided for each brake for each wheel and shall be mounted so that no part of any chamber hangs below the bottom of the axle on which it is mounted.

(2) The service brake shall be capable of providing at least one power-assisted stop with the vehicle engine off that meets the service brake stopping distance standard of Table 2, Performance Parameter 10.

(3) An Anti-Lock Brake System (ABS) shall be provided and included for all wheels.

33. STEERING. All vehicles shall have power-assisted steering.

a. The power assist shall have sufficient capacity so no more than 15 pounds (6.8 kg) pull is necessary on the steering wheel rim to turn the vehicle wheels from lock to lock of the fully loaded vehicle when stationary.

b. The design of the steering mechanism shall permit manual steering to bring the fully loaded vehicle to a safe stop after power-assist failure.

c. The vehicle shall perform as follows when driven on a steering pad around a 100-foot (30 m) radius circle:

(1) With increasing speed, the steering angle shall increase; oversteer is not acceptable.

(2) The vehicle shall remain on the prescribed path until achieving a speed at least equal to the standard specified in Table 2, Performance Parameter 3.

d. The wall-to-wall turning diameter shall be no greater than three times the length of the vehicle.

e. A tilt/telescoping steering wheel/column shall be provided.

34. SUSPENSION.

a. The axles and suspension system shall be such that the total unsprung weight of the vehicle will not be greater than 20 percent of the in-service GVW.

b. Double-acting hydraulic shock absorbers or an equivalent energy-absorbing device shall be provided for all axles or bogies, as applicable.

c. Energy absorbing stops shall be installed so as to prevent damage to axles, drive shafts, the engine oil pan, or any other portions of the chassis from bottoming.

35. TRANSFER CASE.

a. The transfer case shall be certified as suitable for the intended service in accordance with the requirements of Paragraph 103.

b. A transfer case that is either separate or integral with the transmission, shall be acceptable, at the manufacturer's option.

c. A single- or a two-speed transfer case, as required to meet the performance requirements, shall be acceptable, at the manufacturer's option.

d. A transfer case that has either a front axle disconnect, a center differential with automatic or manual lockout, or an overriding clutch to compensate for difference in travel between front and rear wheels, shall be acceptable, at the manufacturer's option.

e. A transfer case that either engages the front and rear axles at all times, engages all axles automatically, or that is driver-operator selectable to engage all-wheel drive and that will not allow the vehicle to stall as long as the tires of engaged axle(s) have traction shall be acceptable, at the manufacturer's option.

36. TRANSMISSION.

a. The transmission shall be certified as suitable for the intended service in accordance with the requirements of Paragraph 103.

b. The transmission shall be a continuous drive system. Either hydrostatic, hydrostatic/automatic, or automatic powershift, incorporating a torque converter with suitable torque ratio, shall be acceptable, at the manufacturer's option. The use of a transfer case to achieve the required performance is acceptable, at the manufacturer's option.

c. The transmission range selector shall have all positions clearly identified and back lit.

d. All drive-line components shall have the same power ratings; i.e., no reduction in transfer through bulkheads.

e. The hydraulic system shall include oil pumps, oil filter and screens, a hydraulic control system, and an oil cooling system capable of limiting the transmission temperature to the maximum recommended by the transmission manufacturer.

f. In addition to meeting the acceleration, gradability, and top speed standards of Paragraphs 51, 55, and 57, the transmission shall have sufficient spacing of intermediate ranges to provide a smooth, uniformly spaced transfer of power over the entire operating range.

37. WHEELS AND TIRE ASSEMBLY.

a. The wheel and tire assembly, including the recommended tire inflation pressure, shall be certified in accordance with Paragraph 103 as being suitable for the intended service.

b. Rim and tire rating shall conform to Federal Motor Vehicle Safety Standards (FMVSS), Standards No. 119 and 120, and applicable tire and rim association recommendations for the type and size of tires furnished.

c. All tires, rims, and wheels shall be identical.

d. The tires shall provide good lateral stability during off-road use in the terrain and climatic conditions expected at the intended airport. They shall also demonstrate safe on-road handling characteristics for operation on wet pavement.

e. Tires shall have a rated capacity at least equal to the load imposed on each tire measured at each wheel at the ground.

f. Tires shall be repairable and replaceable. There shall be a spare tire and wheel/rim assembly provided with, but not mounted on, the vehicle.

NOTE: The principle objective in the selection of the wheel and tire assemblies is to enhance the off-pavement performance on the terrain encountered at the intended airport and, at the same time, meet highway automotive performance standards. However, the off-pavement and overall handling characteristics of a vehicle depend on a number of other factors in addition to tire selection. Additional information to aid the purchaser during specification development, as well as during consultations with the vehicle and tire manufacturers, is provided in Appendix 2.

g. When specified by the purchaser, all tires (including spare) shall include beadlocks. A beadlock press shall also be provided for any quantity of vehicles purchased.

h. All wheels and tires shall be new; retreads are unacceptable for emergency service.

Section 5. Electrical System.

38. COOLANT HEATER. An engine coolant preheating device with thermostat shall be provided, which, at the manufacturer's option, may be of the immersion or circulating type. It shall have sufficient capacity to maintain the engine at the manufacturer's recommended temperature for rapid starting and immediate high initial engine performance.

39. LIGHTING AND MARKING SYSTEM.

a. The lighting and marking system, including reflectors, beacons, and clearance lights, shall satisfy the applicable State and Federal safety standards.

b. The system shall include—

(1) Two or more sealed beam halogen headlights with upper and lower driving beams.

(2) Two spotlights mounted on the roof or high-reach turret.

(3) At least one taillight and one stoplight or one combination taillight/stoplight on each side of the rear of the vehicle in the lower quadrant and a duplicate set of taillight/stoplight in the upper quadrant.

(4) Turn signals, front and rear, with self-canceling control; a visual as well as audible indicator; and a four-way flasher switch.

(5) Reflectors, markers, and clearance lights meeting all applicable FMVSS.

(6) Nonglare-type engine compartment light(s), arranged to illuminate both sides of the engine and with switches(s) located in the engine compartment.

(7) Two backup lights, one installed on each side of the rear of the vehicle.

(8) One or more emergency flashing beacon(s) or strobe(s) as required by vehicle design to meet visibility requirements from the sides, front, and rear of the vehicle. For recognition, the color red shall be used alone or in combination with other colors if it is an operational requirement.

(9) Nonglare-type compartment light(s), arranged to illuminate the inside of all storage, maintenance access, and piping compartments.

c. The purchaser may specify the following options:

(1) Spotlights, quartz lights, fog lights, and area/service lighting.

(2) If, under normal local operational procedures, there are circumstances where it is desirable to identify the status of an ARFF vehicle as other than an ARFF vehicle in emergency response status, at least one amber (yellow) flashing beacon or strobe shall be provided in addition to the requirements of Paragraph 39.b.

40. POWER SUPPLIES.

a. All components such as the alternator, circuit breakers, etc. shall be as waterproof/water resistant as the state-of-the-art permits without the use of marine quality components. They shall be accessibly mounted and protected against exterior and engine heat.

b. One of the following electrical systems shall be provided:

   (1) 12-volt electrical and starting.

   (2) 12-volt electrical/24-volt starting.

   (3) 24-volt electrical and starting.

c. For 12-volt systems, alternators shall be provided that have a minimum curb idle charging rate of 160 amps. For 24-volt systems, an alternator shall be provided that has a minimum curb idle charging rate of 80 amps. In either case, the alternator(s) shall have a total current output capacity adequate to service the full operational electrical load of the vehicle, including all equipment and accessories specified. In addition, a 20-percent reserve alternator capacity shall be provided. The alternator(s) shall have automatic regulation.

NOTE: Provisions to handle the additional load imposed by the winterization kit and/or air conditioning shall be included, when appropriate.

d. A weatherproof, grounded, polarized male plug(s) as required to service the anticipated electrical load, suitable for receiving 110-volts AC from an outside electrical supply, shall be provided.

   (1) The plug(s) shall be mounted as specified by the purchaser.

   (2) The plug(s) shall be wired to a built-in battery conditioner, the engine coolant pre-heating device, and the on-board air compressor, if specified.

   (3) The plug(s) shall be designed to automatically release (auto-eject) as specified by the purchaser.

   (4) The matching female receptacle(s) shall be provided with the vehicle.

e. A battery system shall be provided as follows:

   (1) The system shall contain at least two 12-volt, maintenance free, batteries connected in an approved manner.

   (2) The system shall have sufficient cold cranking battery capacity that meets the engine manufacturer's recommendation for the lowest ambient starting temperature.

   (3) Batteries shall be securely mounted and protected against mechanical damage, water spray, and engine and exhaust heat.

f. If an enclosed battery compartment is provided, it shall be adequately ventilated. The battery connections and the batteries shall be readily accessible for removal and installation, as well as for examination, test, and maintenance. The manufacturer may install roll out trays to provide the required accessibility.

g. A battery charger shall be provided on the vehicle and shall—

   (1) Operate with inputs from 120 or 240 volts AC.

   (2) Be able to supply an uninterrupted source of 12 or 24 volts DC.

   (3) Provide full charge, when needed, to all batteries without interruption or causing any damage. It should have an automatic descending rate of charge input based on the status of the batteries being charged. It should incorporate the capability to descend from a high rate of input to a low rate and totally shut off to prevent overcharge of batteries.

   (4) Be provided with grounded AC receptacle to allow automatic release (auto-eject) connection from an external electrical power supply.

   (5) Have a built-in circuit to protect the battery from deep discharge or from damage during high current demands, such as those caused by starting the engine.

41. STARTER. An electric starting device shall be provided. When operating under maximum load, the current draw shall not cause a voltage drop sufficient to adversely affect the function of other electrical equipment required to operate during the startup process.

42. WIRING.

a. All wiring shall be numbered or color- or function-coded for proper identification. Wiring shall be of stranded conductors and of a wire gauge commensurate with the anticipated maximum electrical load of the circuit.

b. Wires shall be insulated in accordance with the applicable standards of the Society of Automotive Engineers (SAE).

c. All connections shall be made with lugs or terminals mechanically secured to the conductors.

d. Wiring shall be secured in place and protected from heat, oil, lubricants, fire fighting agents, and physical damage. Appropriate circuit breakers shall be provided. Circuit breaker panels shall be easily accessible for service. A diagram and labeling scheme shall be affixed to the inside of the removable or hinged panel cover over the breakers. A copy of this diagram shall also be included in the maintenance manual.

e. Where wiring passes through sheet metal or structural components, rubber grommets shall be used to protect wiring and wiring looms. Precaution must be taken in all areas to guard against chafing or excessive strain.

43. RADIO EQUIPMENT.

a. Provisions shall be made by the purchaser to mount the radio(s) and the associated controls so they are operable by both the driver and at least one other crewmember without leaving the cab or removing their seat belts. The mounting provisions shall take into consideration the fact that radio operating equipment may include boom/microphone headsets with appropriate controls, radio interconnects, and remote or foot-operated push-to-talk switches, as specified by the purchaser. If a vehicle is to be equipped with headsets, storage boxes shall be provided to protect this equipment. The layout of headset controls should allow the headset wires to come from behind the operator so that the wires do not stretch across the cab.

b. Radio mounting locations shall be located so as to—

(1) Not restrict or interfere with the operation of any existing equipment or accessories.

(2) Not restrict cab visibility through the windshield.

(3) Not cause a hazard or obstruction to personnel.

c. The vehicle shall be wired and equipped as follows:

(1) Dedicated radio leads shall be provided to the dash instrument panel and marked and tagged with permanent tags.

(2) The radio power lead(s) shall be provided with circuit protection separately for each.

(3) The radio leads shall be 12 volts, negative ground.

d. The vehicle shall be provided with radio interference protection in accordance with SAE J551/4, Test Limits and Methods of Measurement of Radio Disturbance Characteristics of Vehicles and Devices, Broadband and Narrowband, 150kHz to 1000MHz, or an equivalent radio interference suppression standard.

Section 6. Engine and Accessories.

44. COOLING SYSTEM.

a. The vehicle manufacturer shall certify and provide appropriate documentation in accordance with Paragraphs 100.a(2) and 104 that the complete cooling system installation is suitable for the intended service.

b. The cooling system shall be provided with an automatic thermostat.

c. If a liquid-cooled system is provided, it shall—

(1) Have the capacity to stabilize the engine coolant temperature within the engine manufacturer's prescribed limits under operational conditions at the ambient temperature range normally encountered at the airport.

(2) Have drain cocks installed at the low point of the cooling system and at such other points as may be necessary to drain the system completely.

d. If an air-cooled system is provided, it shall have the capacity to stabilize the cylinder head and oil temperatures within the engine manufacturer's prescribed limits under operational conditions at the ambient temperature range normally encountered at the airport.

e. When provided, radiator or air inlet shutters shall be automatic and "fail safe" in the open position.

f. A cooling system filter/conditioner shall be provided.

45. EXHAUST SYSTEM.

a. The vehicle manufacturer shall certify that the exhaust system is suitable for the intended service.

b. The engine exhaust system shall be constructed of rust-resistant materials and shall be designed and installed so as to prevent the discharge of exhaust toward the ground, engine, or cab air intake or onto vehicle tires. A curved exhaust stack or a straight exhaust pipe with rain cap shall be provided as specified. Exhaust termination requirements that conform with existing Fire Station Diesel Exhaust Entrapment Systems shall be provided, as required.

c. The exhaust system exit shall be located to prevent exhaust gasses from entering the closed cab under all operational conditions and shall include a suitable heavy-duty, commercially available muffler.

d. System components shall be protected from damage that could result from traversing off-road terrain.

e. ARFF vehicle/engines must meet all applicable Federal emission standards and regulations.

46. FUEL SYSTEM.

a. The vehicle manufacturer shall provide a fuel system that meets the engine manufacturer's installation approval and shall certify that the fuel system is suitable for the intended service.

b. All components shall be installed in a protected location or otherwise protected from operational damage, exhaust heat, and exposure to ground fires.

c. The fuel tank(s) shall—

(1) Be constructed of an approved material.

(2) Have an accessible drain plug at the bottom of the fuel tank.

(3) Have a filler pipe (accessible from outside of the cab) that is at least 2.25 inches (5.7 cm) in diameter.

(4) Have sufficient capacity to provide for a minimum of 30 miles (48 km) of highway travel at 45 mph (73km/h) average plus 2 hours of pumping at the full-rated discharge.

(5) Be so located and mounted that it will prevent gravity feed.

d. An approved filter, mounted in an accessible location, shall be provided for each fuel supply line. The fuel supply line filter should be installed in such a manner that allows the free flow fueling of the vehicle without causing back ups and spills.

e. A fuel water separator shall be provided, and heated if specified.

47. GOVERNOR. An engine governor that will not adversely affect the automotive or extinguishing agent system performance shall be provided. The governor shall be set to limit engine speed so that it cannot exceed the maximum rpm recommended by the engine and driveline component manufacturers.

48. LUBRICATION.

a. The engine and transmission shall operate efficiently and without detrimental effect to any drive train components when lubricated with standard, commercially available lubricants in accordance with the recommendations of the engine and transmission manufacturers.

b. The engine oil and transmission fluid filters shall be of the full-flow type with a replaceable spin-on element.

c. All moving parts requiring lubrication shall have a means of providing for such lubrication. There shall be no pressure lubrication fittings where their normal use would damage grease seals or other parts.

d. The vehicle shall be serviced prior to delivery with lubricants, brake and hydraulic fluids, and a cooling system fluid suitable for use in the temperature range expected at the airport.

49. POWER REQUIREMENT.

a. The engine(s) shall be an internal combustion diesel capable of developing the torque and horsepower needed to meet the automotive performance standards in Table 2 and the extinguishing agent discharge performance standards in Table 3. This power requirement shall be achieved without exceeding a "no load" governed speed at the peak of a certified gross brake horsepower (bhp) curve.

b. The engine shall be capable of meeting the specified performance standards while operating on commercial grade diesel fuel.

50. WINTERIZATION–OPTION.

a. Vehicles purchased for use in areas where it is common industrial practice to winterize vehicles shall have a winterization kit installed.

b. The winterization kit shall not detract from the performance of the vehicle or the fire fighting system in ambient temperatures up to 115° F (43.5° C).

c. The winterization kit shall provide sufficient insulation and heating capacity, by means of hot circulating liquids and forced air heat exchangers, to permit satisfactory operation of the vehicle and fire fighting systems for a period of at least 2 hours at ambient temperatures as low as -40° F (-40° C) with the vehicle fully operational and the engine running. At the end of this 2-hour period, the vehicle shall be capable of successfully discharging its agent(s).

Section 7. Automotive Performance.

51. ACCELERATION. Each vehicle shall meet the applicable standard of Table 2, Performance Parameter 9.

52. BRAKE SYSTEM. The stopping and holding performance for each type of brake shall meet the applicable standards of Table 2, Performance Parameters 10, 11, and 12.

53. DYNAMIC AND STATIC STABILITY. The vehicle shall be able to:

a. Pump while rolling in both directions across a 20-percent (12-degree) side slope with extinguishing agents being discharged in any direction of turret azimuth at maximum-rated turret capacity without unanticipated stream interruption or vehicle instability. Pumping capacity shall supply an intermittent discharge, as desired.

b. Remain stationary while headed in either direction across a 20-percent (12-degree) side slope and while the steering is being moved to a maximum turning angle both right and left without any vehicle instability.

c. Meet the applicable side slope stability standard of Table 2, Performance Parameter 2.

d. Meet the applicable dynamic balance standard of Table 2, Performance Parameter 3.

54. ENVIRONMENTAL CONDITIONS. The vehicle shall be capable of withstanding the following conditions without detrimental effect to subsequent operation of the vehicle or any of the fire extinguishing systems:

a. Dust particles, as encountered in desert areas.

b. The corrosive effects of salt fog.

c. Material decay from fungus and mildew.

d. Relative humidity up to 100 percent, as well as wind driven snow, sleet, rain, and vehicle self-splashing of water.

e. Ambient temperature ranging from 32° F to 115° F (0° C to 43.5° C). (See Paragraph 50 for winterization.) If winterization is necessary, the temperature performance range shall extend to at least -40° F (-40° C).

55. GRADABILITY. The vehicle shall be able to—

a. Ascend a smooth, dry, paved road having a 20-percent grade and maintain a speed of at least 8 mph (13 km/h).

b. Ascend, stop, start, and continue ascending and descend, stop, start, and continue descending on a 20-percent grade at a speed of at least 2 mph (3.2 km/h) with extinguishing agents being discharged at maximum-rated capacity from the primary turret(s).

c. Ascend and descend a dry, hard surface incline having a 50-percent grade at not less than 1 mph (1.6 km/h).

d. Climb a vertical wall at least 18 inches (45 cm) high and negotiate terrain that will deflect the opposite wheels of the truck in alternatively contrary directions at least 14 inches (36 cm) without the remaining wheels losing traction.

56. OPERATIONAL RANGE. The fully loaded vehicle shall be able to—

a. Operate continuously for 25 miles (40 km) at speeds up to 60 mph (96 km/h). The test route shall include agricultural lands, paved and unpaved roads, and grades typical of those encountered at the intended airport. During this performance evaluation, the vehicle shall operate in all-wheel drive. At least 5 miles (8 km) of this operation shall be off-road travel.

b. Operate on smooth, dry, level pavement through a range from 1 mph (1.6 km/h) to at least 10 mph (16 km/h) while discharging agents from the primary turret(s) at rated maximum capacity without interruption.

c. Negotiate pooled water to a depth of 2 inches (5 cm) for a distance of at least 150 feet (45 m) at a speed of at least 40 mph (65 km/h) without engine flooding/stalling, loss of directional control, loss of braking, or electrical system(s) shorting.

d. Operate for 10 minutes on dry, paved roadway at not more than 2 mph (3.2 km/h) at an engine speed that does not result in rough, irregular operation.

e. Ascend a dry, paved incline having an 8-percent grade for a distance of 0.25 mile (0.4 km) at a speed of not less than 20 mph (32 km/h).

f. Negotiate (J Turn) a 90-degree, 150-foot radius turn at 30 mph (48 km/h) on smooth, dry, level pavement without loss of directional control or stability.

57. TOP SPEED. The vehicle shall be able to consistently reach a top speed of 65 mph (104 km/h) and maintain a constant speed of at least 60 mph (96 km/h) on typical paved, level (grades of less than 1 percent) highway surfaces for a minimum distance of 20 miles (32 km) without showing overheat symptoms in any portion of the cooling system or power train.

58. OFF-ROAD HIGH-MOBILITY SUSPENSIONS.

a. An off-road, high-mobility suspension system resulting in no more than 0.5 g rms acceleration at the seat of the vehicle when traversing an 8-inch (24 cm) half round at 35 mph (56 km/h) shall be provided. Such suspension systems include, but are not limited to, independent, passive struts, semi-active, active/reactive, and articulated.

b. If specified by the purchaser, the system shall include a central tire inflation/deflation system supporting an off-road response at 35 mph (56 km/h) when operating within the runway safety area over similar terrain near the improved surface areas of the airfield. Typically, this area has been moderately graded, has had most major obstructions removed, and has a sod cover.

59. DRIVER'S ENHANCED VISION SYSTEM (DEVS). DEVS equipment can aid normal operations and provide an additional margin of safety for airport rescue response during periods of very low-visibility operations. DEVS equipment improves emergency response time during periods of low visibility, reduces the probability of secondary accidents often associated with poor weather and low-visibility conditions, and improves command and control in the event of an aircraft incident or accident. A complete DEVS comprises three subsystems: night vision, navigation, and tracking. The provision of each subsystem shall be subject to the criteria below. Because of the complexity of a DEVS, procurement and installation may be optional and by separate contract and shall comply with AC 150/5210-19, Driver's Enhanced Vision System (DEVS).

a. **Night vision.** The purpose of the night vision subsystem is to improve the ARFF vehicle driver's ability to see at night and through smoke, fog, and adverse weather; it consists of a Forward Looking InfraRed (FLIR) camera and a minimum 10-inch monitor in the cab. This subsystem shall be provided on all vehicles.

b. **Navigation.** Using a differential GPS and a moving map display inside the cab, the navigation subsystem shows ARFF vehicle drivers their location, the accident site, and the path between to ensure rapid advance toward the site. When the airport is required to have a Surface Movement Guidance and Control System (SMGCS), the purchaser may specify the addition of this system. If specified, it shall be compatible with an existing tracking subsystem.

c. **Tracking.** The vehicle tracking subsystem allows an overview of all vehicles at the command center and provides reliable digital communications with vehicles. It is composed of a display at the command center and a digital radio datalink between the command center and vehicles. This subsystem shall be provided when the airport is required to have a SMGCS, the subsystem does not presently exist at the airport, and it is specified by the purchaser.

60. THROUGH 69. RESERVED.

Table 2. Automotive Performance Standards

PERFORMANCE PARAMETER FOR FULLY LOADED VEHICLE	VEHICLE CLASS	
	1	2
1. Minimum Rated Water Capacity (gallons):	1,500	3,000 and over

2.   Side Slope Stability:
     Degrees
 	
     Percent Grade
	30°
	
	58%
		30°
		
		58%

3. Dynamic Balance: Minimum Speed on 100-foot Radius Circle (mph)	22	22
4. Approach and Departure: Angles	30°	30°
5. Interaxle Clearance: Angle	12°	12°
6. Underbody Clearance:	18"	18"
7. Underaxle Clearance at Differential Housing Bowl:	13"	13"
8. Wall-to-Wall Turning Diameter:	Less than 3 x vehicle length	
9. Maximum Acceleration Time from 0 to 50 mph (seconds):	25	35

10.   Service Brake:
    Stopping Distance from: 20 mph
                            40 mph
	Maximum 35'
	Maximum 131'
		40'
		160'

Hold Fully Loaded Vehicle:	Minimum 50% grade Ascending and Descending	
11. Emergency Brake: Stopping Distance from 40 mph	Maximum 288'	
12. Parking Brake: Hold Fully Loaded Vehicle	Minimum 20% grade Ascending or Descending	
13. Evasive Maneuver Test (NATO Lane Change):	35 mph	
14. J-Turn Test: 90-degree, 150-foot Radius Turn	30mph	

Table 2M. Automotive Performance Standards (Metric)

PERFORMANCE PARAMETER FOR FULLY LOADED VEHICLE		VEHICLE CLASS	
		1	2
1.	Minimum Rated Water Capacity (liters):	5,685	11,370 and over
2.	Side Slope Stability:		
	Degrees	30°	30°
	Percent Grade	58%	58%
3.	Dynamic Balance: Minimum Speed on 30-meter Radius Circle (km/h)	35	35
4.	Approach and Departure: Angles	30°	30°
5.	Interaxle Clearance: Angle	12°	12°
6.	Underbody Clearance (cm):	46	46
7.	Underaxle Clearance at Differential Housing Bowl (cm):	33	33
8.	Wall-to-Wall Turning Diameter:	Less than 3 x vehicle length	
9.	Maximum Acceleration Time from 0 to 80 km/h (seconds):	25	35
10.	Service Brake: Stopping Distance from: 32 km/h 64 km/h	Maximum 11 m Maximum 40 m	14 m 48 m
	Hold Fully Loaded Vehicle:	Minimum 50% grade Ascending and Descending	
11.	Emergency Brake: Stopping Distance from 64 km/h	Maximum 86 m	
12.	Parking Brake: Hold Fully Loaded Vehicle	Minimum 20% grade Ascending or Descending	
13.	Evasive Maneuver Test (NATO Lange Change):	56km/h	
14.	J-Turn Test: 90-degree, 46-meter Radius Turn	48km/h	

CHAPTER 3. FIRE EXTINGUISHING SYSTEMS.

Section 1. Dry Chemical–Option.

70. AGENT CONTAINER(S) AND COMPONENTS.

    a.　The dry chemical container(s) shall—

    (1)　Be constructed and stamped in accordance with the American Society of Mechanical Engineers (ASME) Code for Unfired Pressure Vessels.

    (2)　Be certified in accordance with Paragraph 103.c.

    (3)　Be able to hold at least 450 usable pounds (204 kg) of a potassium-based dry chemical fire extinguishing agent.

    (4)　Have an accessible fill opening that is easy to open and close and be provided with a compatible funnel to permit filling from dry chemical storage containers. The overall design shall allow filling without the removal of any of the extinguisher piping or any major component other than the fill cap.

    (5)　Have a pressure relief device conforming to appropriate ASME codes that will protect both the container and the low-pressure piping.

    (6)　Include a gauge that indicates the pressure in the agent container at all times.

    b.　A check valve shall be provided in the gas piping to prevent the agent from being forced back into the propellant gas line.

    c.　A quick-acting agent system activation control shall be accessible to the seated driver and at least one other crew position. A similar control shall be located near the agent handline.

    d.　The agent pressurization system shall ensure fluidization of the dry chemical at the time of activation. Designs that include the automatic movement of the chemical or chemical container to help fluidize the contents shall also include a manual operating feature.

    e.　There shall be provisions for purging agent from all piping and hose after use without discharging the remaining chemical. Also, there shall be provisions for the depressurization of the chemical container without the loss of the remaining chemical.

    f.　Dash pressure gauges shall be installed that, when the system is activated, will allow the vehicle operator to determine the propellant reservoir status as well as the system operating pressure.

71. AGENT DELIVERY PIPING AND VALVES.

    a.　The piping, couplings, and valves shall be sized to provide the gas flow into the system and the agent flow out of the chemical container needed to meet the requirements of Table 3, Performance Parameter 1.a and b.

    b.　All piping and fittings shall conform to the appropriate ASME code. The completed system shall be designed and installed so as to withstand the recommended working pressure of the system.

    c.　The integrity of the installed discharge piping shall be tested at a pressure equal to 150 percent of the system working pressure.

    d.　Material for all piping, couplings, and valves shall be resistant to agent, weather, and galvanic corrosion.

    e.　Piping shall be securely mounted and provided with flexible couplings where needed to minimize stress.

    f.　When more than one agent discharge outlet is provided, the size and design of piping, pressure regulators, and fittings shall provide design flow to each outlet.

    g.　All valves shall be of the quarter-turn type, selected for ease of operation and freedom from leaks.

72. PROPELLANT, PROPELLANT CONTAINERS, AND COMPONENTS.

    a.　The propellant gas shall be either dry nitrogen or dry air. Sufficient container capacity shall be provided to ensure enough gas to discharge all of the agent and to permit purging of all pipes and hose lines after use.

    b.　All propellant gas cylinders and valves shall comply with U.S. Department of Transportation (DOT) requirements. Cylinders shall bear the DOT marking, including evidence of a current hydrostatic test and shall be certified in accordance with Paragraph 103.f.

c.   In addition to the provisions in Paragraph 70 f, pressure gauges shall be provided on the agent tank and propellant tank that will indicate the pressure on the propellant gas system downstream of the pressure regulator and in the propellant cylinder at all times.

d.   Cylinder valves, gauges, and piping shall be arranged or protected to preclude accidental mechanical damage during fire fighting operations.

e.   The pressure reduction system shall automatically reduce the normal storage cylinder pressure to (and hold it at) the designed operating pressure of the dry chemical container. The regulator may be of a type without pressure indicating gauges.

(1) Pressure regulating devices shall be equipped with a spring-loaded relief valve that will relieve any excess pressure that may develop in the regulator.

(2) All pressure regulating devices shall be sealed or pinned at the designed operating pressures after final adjustment by the system manufacturer and shall be certified in accordance with Paragraph 103.g.

(3) Regulators must be of a high-flow variety that allows a rapid buildup time for system pressure for a full system charge and operation.

f.   A device shall be provided that allows for servicing the propellant cylinder by one person from ground level. The purchaser may specify that the device be manual or electric.

Section 2. Clean Agent–Option

73. AGENT CONTAINER AND COMPONENTS.

a.   The container material shall be suitable for the storage of Clean Agent and shall be constructed in accordance with ASME Code for Unfired Pressure Vessels and stamped. The container shall have—

(1) A capacity of at least 460 pounds of Clean Agent.

(2) A fill coupling of sufficient size to allow agent tank filling without loss of agent. It shall permit tank filling without the removal/disconnection of any piping or major components. The fill coupling shall be provided with a dust cap secured to the coupling with a safety chain.

(3) A means of determining the contents of the container as a guide in recharging partial loads and to prevent overfilling of the tank.

(4) A gauge that indicates the pressure in the agent container at all times.

b.   A means of pressure relief conforming to appropriate ASME codes shall be provided for the chemical container and piping. A check valve shall be provided in the gas piping to prevent agent from being forced back into the propellant gas line.

c.   The manufacturer shall make provisions for the purging of agent from the discharge piping and hose without discharging the chemical remaining in the container and for the depressurization of the chemical container without the loss of the remaining chemical.

74. AGENT DELIVERY PIPING AND VALVES.

a.   The piping, couplings, and valves shall be sized to provide the gas flow into the system and the agent flow out of the chemical container needed to meet the requirements of Table 3, Performance Parameter 2.

b.   The applicable requirements of Paragraph 71.b through 71.g also apply.

75. PROPELLANT, PROPELLANT CONTAINERS, AND COMPONENTS.
The requirements of Paragraph 72 also apply.

Section 3. Foam Concentrate System.

76. CONCENTRATE PROPORTIONER.

a. A foam concentrate proportioning system shall be provided to control the ratio of foam concentrate to water in the water/foam solution being discharged from all orifices normally used for ARFF operations.

(1) The proportioning system for a 6-percent concentrate shall be sufficiently accurate to provide for the discharge of finished foam within the range of 5.5-percent to 7-percent foam concentrate in the discharged water/foam solution.

(2) If a foam concentrate other than 6 percent is used, the precision range shall be modified in direct ratio. Thus, a 3-percent concentrate shall be in the 2.8- to 3.5-percent concentrate range in the discharged solution.

b. This precision shall be maintained for all individual discharges and for the maximum simultaneous discharge rate of all turrets, handlines, and ground sweeps while delivering the quantity of concentrate required to meet the agent discharge requirements of Table 3.

77. CONCENTRATE RESERVOIR AND PIPING.

a. Materials used in reservoir construction and piping shall be compatible with the foam concentrate, the water/foam solution, and water and shall not be subject to corrosive or acidic reaction caused by foam concentrate or water.

b. A rigid or a flexible foam concentrate reservoir shall be acceptable, at the manufacturer's option.

(1) If the reservoir is separate from the water tank, the mounting of the reservoir shall limit the transfer of torsional strains from the chassis to the reservoir.

(2) The reservoir shall be separate and distinct from the crew compartment, engine compartment, and chassis and removable as a unit.

(3) The reservoir(s) shall have a working capacity sufficient for two tanks of water based on the percent foam concentrate used at the airport.

(4) Flexible reservoirs shall be supported in a manner that does not depend on the fluid level in either the foam or water reservoirs for its structural integrity.

(5) For other than lifetime warranted tanks, provisions shall be made for access for internal and external inspection and service. Reservoirs large enough to require baffles shall be provided with access to each baffled compartment.

(6) The reservoir shall be fitted with a sump, complete with antiswirl baffles, and a 1.5-inch (38 mm) minimum diameter drain with a valve and an accessible control.

(7) The reservoir outlet(s) shall be located above the bottom of the sump and shall permit a continuous flow of foam concentrate to the proportioning system with that system supporting the discharge standards of Table 3 during the discharge of two consecutive tanks of water.

(8) Reservoirs shall be vented to permit the required fill rate without exceeding the design working pressure and to permit emptying at the maximum design flow rate without danger of collapse. The vent outlets shall prevent spillage of foam concentrate on vehicle components.

c. The fill system shall be capable of delivering foam concentrate to the reservoir at a rate at least equal to the maximum use rate of the foam proportioning system.

(1) The bottom fill connection shall be provided and shall be no more than 60 inches (150 cm) from the ground. The inlet shall be fitted with stainless steel strainers of 1/4-inch (6 mm) mesh and shall have check valves or be so constructed that no more than 0.25 gal (1l) of foam is lost from the reservoir during connection or disconnection of the foam resupply line. An isolation valve shall be installed on the foam line as it leaves the tank to allow easy maintenance on foam plumbing.

(2) A top fill opening shall be provided and equipped with a No. 10 gauge mesh, corrosion resistant (stainless steel or equal) screen, and a 5-gallon agent container opener to permit the rapid emptying of 5-gallon containers into the reservoir(s). The fill line from the trough shall introduce foam concentrate into the reservoir so as to minimize foaming.

d. The foam concentrate piping shall be sized to permit the flow rates needed to meet the agent discharge requirements of Table 3 and shall be arranged to prevent water from entering the foam reservoir.

e. The foam concentrate piping shall be so arranged that the entire system, including any foam concentrate pumps, can be flushed with water from the water tank without contaminating the foam reservoir.

Section 4. Water System.

78. PIPING, COUPLINGS, CONNECTIONS, AND VALVES.

a. A pressure relief valve shall be fitted to the discharge system that is set to ensure discharge standards can be met and that surges above the designed operating pressure are relieved.

b. Hose connections shall have National (American) Standard fire hose coupling threads.

EXCEPTION: Adapters, securely attached to each outlet, shall be acceptable if local couplings do not meet National (American) Standards as specified in NFPA 1963, Standard for Screw Threads and Gaskets for Fire Hose Connections, and the outlet(s) with adapters do not add to the width or length of the vehicle.

c. All water system piping on the suction side of the pump shall be tested to detect leaks. All water and foam solution discharge piping, together with the agent pump(s), shall be tested at 150 percent of the normal system operating pressure.

d. If two pumps are used, they shall be arranged in parallel with a manifold so that either or both may supply any discharge outlet at the required operating pressure. During single pump operation, total discharge capacity may be proportionally reduced.

e. Piping, couplings, and valves shall be sized to provide agent flow to all discharge devices operating to the applicable standards of Table 3.

f. A drain shall be provided in the suction system at the lowest point with a valve for draining all of the liquid from the pumping system.

g. A drainage system, with collector tubing from the low points on pump(s) and piping, shall be provided.

h. All valves shall be selected for ease of operation and leak-free design.

i. Material for all piping, couplings, and valves shall be selected to avoid corrosion.

j. Piping shall be securely mounted and provided with flexible couplings to minimize stress from chassis flexing. Union, gasketed, or fittings shall be provided where required to facilitate removal of piping.

k. The purchaser may specify a limited structural exterior panel, which includes—

(1) Engine instruments and pump controls, including a tachometer, an oil pressure gauge, a temperature gauge, and a pressure control; pump shift; manual metering control; two compound suction-pressure gauges; water tank isolation valve; and panel lights.

(2) Either one or two 2-1/2-inch discharged valves shall be provided. Each discharge valve shall be provided with pressure gauge and bleeder. One manual metering control shall be provided.

(3) One 2-1/2-inch and one large diameter suction inlet connection with bleeder shall be provided, if specified.

l. A priming pump and reservoir shall be provided if specified.

79. WATER PUMPS AND PUMP DRIVE.

a. The water pump drive, if common with the vehicle drive, shall have sufficient power to meet the automotive performance and water/foam agent discharge standards of Tables 2 and 3, individually and simultaneously, as applicable.

b. If an independent pump engine is used, it shall—

(1) Have fuel, electrical, lubrication, hydraulic, and coolant requirements that are compatible with the chassis engine.

(2) Have sufficient power capacity to meet the water/foam agent discharge standards of Table 3 under all normal vehicle operational modes and environmental conditions.

(3) Be certified by the manufacturer as suitable for the intended service.

c. The water pump(s) shall—

(1) Have sufficient capacity to supply the water/foam solution at the pressures and volumes required to simultaneously fulfill the discharge standards of Table 3.

(2) Be a centrifugal type. The manufacturer may provide either single- or multiple-stage pumps.

(3) Be gravity primed from the vehicle reservoir, regardless of the water level in the tank. The associated piping shall be designed and installed so as to prevent air lock.

EXCEPTION: If design considerations require the water pump to be mounted above the bottom of the water tank, it shall have an automatic priming system and provisions shall be made to prevent the loss of prime during intermittent pumping operations, particularly when the water level falls below the pump inlet level.

(4) Be constructed of materials that are compatible with water, water/foam solutions, and foam concentrate. If specified, a bronze water pump shall be supplied if local water conditions require additional protection from corrosive, acidic, or saltwater conditions.

d. The design, construction, and installation of the pump, pump drive system, and associated piping and controls shall—

(1) Allow the vehicle motive drive to be engaged while pumping operations are in progress without damage to or lurching of the vehicle.

(2) Permit the engagement of the pump at any engine and vehicle speed combination encountered during a normal vehicle operations profile.

(3) Allow pump engagement during vehicle operations, without engine stall and without causing more than a slight and momentary reduction in the engine speed, or damage to any of the components.

e. The manufacturer shall provide a means of automatically preventing the water pump and, if applicable, the foam pump from overheating while engaged and operating at zero discharge.

80. WATER RESERVOIR AND PIPING.

a. The water reservoir shall—

(1) Have a minimum rated capacity (working capacity) that meets the water quantity standard presented in Table 3, Performance Parameter 7.

(2) Be constructed of material suitable (i.e., stainless steel, bronze, brass or stainless steel flexible material) for service with the water intended to be used by the purchaser.

(3) Have sufficient longitudinal and transverse baffles with baffle openings that are not in-line.

(4) Be equipped, for other than lifetime warranted tanks, with removable manhole covers, plates, or removable tops to permit access to the sump.

(5) Be fitted with a sump, complete with antiswirl baffles, a 2.5-inch (6.5 cm) main water tank drain and another low-point drain as required, an isolation valve, and a quarter-turn valve that has an accessible handle.

(6) Have a top-fill opening diameter of at least 8 inches (20 cm), a screen with maximum ¼-inch (6.4 mm) mesh, and a gasketed, latchable cap.

(7) Be vented to permit filling and overfilling at the rate specified in Paragraph 80.c and discharging in accordance with Table 3 without exceeding the design operating pressure or causing the reservoir to collapse. Overflow shall be directed to the ground.

(8) Have one 2.5-inch water tank fill connection with bleeder valve for Class 1 vehicles and one 4.5–inch tank fill connection with 4-inch plumbing valve with a 4.5-inch X 2.5-inch reducer with cap for Class 2 vehicles. The purchaser shall specify the size of thread connections.

b. The discharge piping shall be sized to allow sufficient water to the pump for the simultaneous operation of all turrets, ground sweeps, handlines, and undertruck nozzles, at the applicable discharge rates specified in Table 3.

c. Each connection and corresponding fill piping shall be sized to permit filling in no more than 2 minutes when the supply source provides sufficient volume at 80 psi (5.5 Bar) at the reservoir fill connection. If required, the capability of filling the water tank directly by drafting shall be provided.

Section 5. Handlines, Reels, and Compartments.

81. HANDLINES.

a. There shall be a minimum of two handlines with nozzles for the discharge of water/foam that may be of the woven jacket or reeled type as specified by the purchaser. Reeled swing-out type hoses are acceptable, at the purchaser's option. These handlines are to be located on either side (front or rear) or at the rear of the vehicle. If a complementary agent system is provided, the handline shall be "twinned" with one or both of the reeled water/foam handlines as specified by the purchaser. If a twin agent handline is specified for a dry chemical system, a nozzle that will entrain or capture dry chemical within the master stream of water agent flow may be provided if specified by the purchaser.

b. If selected by the purchaser, the reeled complementary and water/foam handlines shall—

(1) Be able to meet the discharge performance standard of Table 3, Performance Parameter 3, with the hose fully unrolled.

(2) Have at least 150 feet (45 m) of hose on each water/foam reel or each dedicated complementary agent reel. A complementary twinned agent reel shall have at least 100 feet (30 m) of hose.

(3) Be equipped with a variable pattern, pistol-grip shutoff-type nozzle that meets the discharge and pattern performance standard of Table 3, Performance Parameter 3, for both water and foam and be certified to meet NFPA 1964, Standard for Spray Nozzles and Tips.

(4) Electric rewind shall be provided for each hose reel.

c. If selected by the purchaser, the woven jacket water/foam handlines shall—

(1) Be able to meet the discharge performance standard of Table 3, Performance Parameter 4, with the hose fully stretched.

(2) Have at least 150 feet (45 m) of hose in each handline.

(3) Be equipped with a variable pattern, pistol-grip shutoff-type nozzle that meets the discharge and pattern performance standard of Table 3, Performance Parameter 4, for both water and foam and be certified to meet NFPA 1964.

(4) Meet the requirements of NFPA 1961, Standard for Fire Hose.

(5) Be stored and preconnected in a hose compartment.

NOTE: See the "NOTE" following Paragraph 110.d.(13) for a clarification of the handline test discharge rate conditions.

d. If selected by the purchaser, each pre-connected handline shall be equipped with a system that will allow it to be advanced when the pump pressure is at minimum, where the pump rpm will advance only after the nozzle(s) is opened and return again to low rpm when flow is stopped for standby operation to prevent pump overheat and damage. This system shall not eliminate or override the normal pumping mode controls in the cab.

82. WOVEN JACKET HOSE AND REEL HOSE COMPARTMENTS.

a. Each woven jacket hose compartment shall—

(1) Have capacity for at least 150 feet (45 m) of 1.50-inch (38 mm) or 1.75-inch (44 mm) multiple jacket hose, as specified.

(2) Be fabricated from corrosion-resistant material and designed and constructed to drain by gravity.

(3) Be smooth and free from all projections that might damage the hose.

(4) Have no other equipment mounted or located where it will obstruct the removal of the hose.

(5) Be not more than 6 feet (1.8 m) above the ground unless installed on a reel.

(6) Have located in or adjacent to it a manually operated quarter-turn ball-type valve that controls the flow to each handline.

(7) Be weathertight and fitted with a closure that can be secured in either the open or closed position.

(8) Be stored on a roll out tray, which will maximize compartment storage space. The purchaser may also specify that the manufacturer provide an adjustable shelf with roll out tray in the upper part of

each pre-connected hose compartment, above the stored hose.

b. Each hose reel shall—

(1) Be positioned to permit hose line removal by one person from any position in a 120-degree horizontal sector in front of the reel.

(2) Be equipped with a friction brake that will prevent the hose from unrolling when the vehicle is in motion.

(3) Be equipped with a power rewind with manual override.

(4) Have located adjacent to it a manually operated, quarter-turn, ball-type valve that controls the flow to each handline.

c. Each hose reel compartment shall—

(1) Be provided with hose rollers on the left, right, and bottom edges of the reel compartment.

(2) Be weathertight and fitted with a closure that can be secured in either the open or closed position.

Section 6. Turrets, Man-rated Aerials, and Undertruck Nozzles.

83. PRIMARY TURRET. A primary turret can be either a roof or bumper turret.

a. One primary turret that meets the discharge and pattern standards of Table 3, Performance Parameter 5, shall be provided. It shall—

(1) Rotate at least 90 degrees to either side of center.

(2) Have a total traverse of at least 180 degrees.

(3) Elevate at least 45 degrees above the horizontal.

(4) Be capable of both high- and low-flow agent distribution and include a means of indicating to the driver/operator which flow rate is being distributed.

(5) Be fitted with nozzles that entrain or capture dry chemical application within the master stream of water agent flow if a dry chemical discharge from the primary turret is specified.

(6) Be operated with power-assist or as otherwise specified.

b. Roof-mounted turrets (optional flow) may have flow rates reduced by 200 gpm if the ground bumper turret flow rate is increased by the same amount.

c. Where the turret control is in the cab, operating forces shall be less than 30 pounds (13.5 kg).

A device to indicate turret azimuth and elevation shall be provided.

d. Turrets with a flow rate of 500 gpm (1.893 l/min) or more shall permit selection of either 50 percent or 100 percent of the rated turret discharge.

84. SECONDARY TURRET. A secondary turret can be either a roof or bumper turret. A power joystick controlled secondary turret shall be provided that meets the discharge and pattern standards of Table 3, Performance Parameter 6. It shall—

a. Have controls located in the cab within easy reach of the driver and a second crewmember.

b. Rotate 90 degrees to either side of center.

c. Have a total traverse of at least 180 degrees.

d. Elevate at least 45 degrees above the horizontal.

e. Be capable of automatic oscillation through a total traverse of at least 180 degrees with controls to adjust the oscillation angles, where specified by the purchaser.

85. HIGH-REACH EXTENDABLE TURRET–OPTION. There are many advantages to the high-reach extendable turret. It allows firefighters to position their primary turret in an attack position, which will provide the most efficient use of agent. This position may range from ground level to a high-mounted engine or to the fuselage. The discharge of agent can begin while the vehicle is moving. A high-reach turret can be provided with penetrating nozzles as well as systems to discharge secondary agents.

a. If selected as the primary turret by the purchaser, the device provided shall—

(1) Meet the requirements of NFPA 1901, Standard for Automotive Fire Apparatus, latest edition. It shall achieve an 11-degree (20-percent) side slope with the extendable turret fully elevated and the nozzle rotated uphill at maximum horizontal rotation while discharging at maximum flow rate.

(2) Meet the functional requirements of Paragraph 84.a, b, and c for a conventional roof turret.

(3) Meet the primary water/foam agent turret discharge requirements of Table 3A, Performance Parameter 2, for high flow and Performance Parameter 3 for low flow, while in the bedded position.

(4) Meet the foam quality standards of Table 4 for the applicable foam applicator and foam type.

(5) Function during ARFF operations without the need for outriggers or other ground contact stabilizers that would render the vehicle immobile or hinder its maneuverability.

(6) Achieve the elevation and reach needed to service the highest tail-mounted engine for the type of aircraft specified by the purchaser and start application of agent within 30 seconds of activating the deployment cycle. The high-rise, telescoping, and/or articulating movement of the boom/tower shall be accomplished with not more than two adjacent lever controls and may be manual or automated, as specified by the purchaser, for preselected positioning of the elevation and reach. If automated, these functions shall be provided with a manual override positioning capability. All elevated and extendable turret should have an "auto-bed" feature.

(7) Be capable of applying agent to the upper level interior area of the most current wide body jet, height of 34 feet (10 m) from ground, with the vehicle positioned a horizontal distance of 20 feet (6 m) from the side of the aircraft so as not to impede evacuation or endanger the vehicle operator. In addition, the device must be capable of positioning the nozzle assembly at or near ground level at a minimum of 15 feet (4.5 m) in front of vehicle and be capable of applying an agent to the interior of the aircraft through cargo bay openings, passenger doorways, and emergency exits on the type

of aircraft, while the aircraft is in either the gear-up or gear-down landing position.

(8) Have a range of motion so as to permit positioning of the nozzle to direct a fire fighting agent stream at least 90 degrees to the longitudinal axis of the fuselage for interior fire extinguishment.

(9) Be capable of providing for horizontal movement of the boom along the aircraft of at least 30 degrees left and right of the vehicle centerline so as not to require repositioning or movement of the ARFF vehicle, including yellow flashing light to indicate to the operator when rotation exceeds 15 degrees. This horizontal rotation must be accomplished without the deployment of stabilizers or outriggers that might cause a delay in positioning or emergency movement of the rescue vehicle.

(10) Have sufficient backup systems to allow for override of the single-lever boom control and hydraulic system (or other power source) if the primary system becomes disabled.

(11) If the vehicle is provided with a dry chemical discharge, be fitted with nozzles that entrain or capture dry chemical application within the master stream of water agent flow if specified by the purchaser.

b. If specified by the purchaser as both a primary water/foam and a dry chemical turret (i.e., to function as a dual-agent turret system), the device shall meet the agent discharge performance of Table 3, Item 8.a, b, and c while in the bedded position.

c. For non-man-rated devices, the purchaser may specify either an adjustable or dual flow rate nozzle that will allow flow rates and patterns suitable for interior aircraft fire fighting.

d. Requirements for non-man-rated aerials (high-reach turrets) have advantages during initial response where fast knockdown and penetration of the fuselage are critical to the mission. If a non-man-rated device is specified by the purchaser, it shall have the tools and devices needed for a driver or another operator to remotely perform the interior aircraft and tail-mounted engine fire fighting functions. The following are examples of such tools/devices:

(1) If specified, an auxiliary agent line capable of discharging either dry chemical or Clean Agent or approved equivalent through an appropriate nozzle while the device is extended out and up to its maximum operational reach. It shall meet the minimum auxiliary agent flow rate and pattern requirements of Table 3A.

(2) Remote optics capable of sufficient resolution to permit overall fire scene surveillance when fully extended and to provide the driver/operator with the detail needed for placement of the penetration device on the aircraft hull for proper piercing. The camera and associated lighting shall be designed and installed for exterior environmental operating conditions normally encountered by ARFF vehicles. A monitor (10 inches or larger) shall be cab-mounted in a road-worthy manner and readily accessible to the driver/operator.

(3) Skin penetrator/agent applicator—for penetration of the fuselage to access passenger cabin or cargo compartment fires from outside the aircraft. It shall be moveable in conjunction with the water/foam nozzle to allow proper placement with the nozzle control. It shall have a minimum flow requirement of 250 gpm (948 l/m).

(4) A roof window or observation window that allows the cab occupants to see the high-reach extendible turret device from their seated positions if the cab design precludes such observation. This window shall be transparent or lightly tinted to reduce glare. It shall not interfere with the range or operation of the high-reach extendible turret or any other existing components. The window shall be protected or guarded from damage by the operation or bedding of the high-reach device.

86. MAN-RATED AERIALS. For airports servicing wide-body aircraft, which have adequate garaging facilities and sufficient staffing, man-rated aerial devices provide certain abilities offered by no other ARFF apparatus. Man-rated aerials provide safe stable platforms for personnel and equipment during fire fighting operations and a means of gaining access to aircraft or high-mounted engines and other high-mounted aircraft positions and systems.

a. If a man-rated device is specified by the purchaser, access and load ratings shall allow a properly equipped firefighter to use the tools and water/foam or auxiliary agent handlines necessary to perform the functions associated with interior aircraft fire fighting and fight tail-mounted engine fires from the fully extended device. Tip load rating shall be a minimum of 500 pounds (225 kg) as determined by NFPA 1901. If the device is equipped with a ladder attached to the boom or sections for continuous egress, it shall meet the requirements of NFPA 1901.

b. When specified by the purchaser, a man-rated aerial shall be equipped with adjustable or dual flow rate nozzle that will allow flow rates and patterns suitable for interior aircraft fire fighting. If provided, the nozzle shall be adjustable or dual flow rate at the manufacturer's option.

c. If a man-rated aerial is specified by the purchaser, it shall meet the requirements of NFPA 1901.

87. DUAL AGENT TURRET. If a dual-agent turret is specified by the purchaser, it shall—

a. Meet the applicable discharge and pattern standards of Table 3, Performance Parameters 5 and 8.

b. Be capable of being depressed to discharge water/foam agent to within 30 feet (9 m) of the front bumper of the vehicle at full output using a dispersed stream.

c. If specified by the purchaser, a nozzle that entrains or captures dry chemical within the master stream of the water agent flow shall be provided.

88. UNDERTRUCK NOZZLES. If specified by the purchaser, a minimum of three (3) water/foam undertruck nozzles shall be provided so that the combined spray pattern will cover the total undertruck area as well as the inner sides of the wheels and tires.

Section 7. Agent System Performance.

89. COMPLEMENTARY AGENT SYSTEM–OPTION.

a. If a dry chemical system is specified by the purchaser, it shall meet the standards of Table 3, Performance Parameter 1.

b. If a Clean Agent or approved equivalent substitute system is specified by the purchaser, it shall meet the standards of Table 3, Performance Parameter 2.

90. WATER/FOAM AGENT APPLICATORS.

a. Each water/foam agent handline shall be capable of delivering a finished foam solution that meets the applicable rate, range, and pattern standards of Table 3, Performance Parameters 3 or 4.

b. Each water/foam agent handline shall deliver finished foam of a quality that meets the applicable standards of Table 4.

c. Each water/foam agent turret shall be capable of delivering a finished foam solution that meets the applicable rate, range, and pattern standards of Table 3, Performance Parameters 5 or 6, as applicable.

d. Each water/foam agent turret shall deliver a finished foam of a quality that meets the applicable standards of Table 4.

All water/foam applicator performance requirements are based on the assumption that foam used to perform the tests is an approved foam concentrate; e.g., will pass the military AFFF foam specification 50 ft² fire test and the burnback resistance test.

91. THROUGH 99. RESERVED.

Table 3. Extinguishing Agent System Performance Standards.

AGENT SYSTEM PERFORMANCE PARAMETER	VEHICLE CLASS	
	1	2

1. Dry Chemical Handline:
  a. Discharge Rate
  b. Range
	$\geq$ 5 lbs per sec $\leq$ 7 lbs per sec
	At least 25 feet	

2. Clean Agent or Approved Equivalent Handline:
  a. Discharge Rate
  b. Range
	$\geq$ 5 lbs per sec $\leq$ 7 lbs per sec
	At least 25 feet	

3. Reeled Water/Foam Handline:
  a. Nozzle Flow Rate: $\pm$ 5%
  b. Straight Stream Pattern
  c. Dispersed Stream Pattern
	$\geq$ 60 gpm (or 95gpm for 1.25-in. i.d. hose)
	$\geq$ 50 ft reach
	$\geq$ 20 ft reach and $\geq$ 15 ft wide	

4. Woven Jacket Water/Foam Handline:
  a. Nozzle Flow Rate: $\pm$5%
  b. Straight Stream Pattern
  c. Dispersed Stream Pattern
	$\geq$ 125 gpm or lower as specified
	$\geq$ 65 ft reach
	$\geq$ 20 ft reach and $\geq$ 15 ft wide	

5. Primary Turret Discharge:
  a. Flow Rate (gpm): (-0%, +10%)
  b. Stream Pattern/Distances:
    (1) Straight/Far Point (ft)
    (2) Dispersed/Far Point (ft)
    (3) Dispersed/Width (ft)
	750
	
	190
	65
	35
		1,200
		
		250
		75
		35

6. Secondary Turret:
  a. Flow Rate (gpm): (-0%, +10%)
  b. Flat Patter Distances:
    (1) Near Point
 	
    (2) Width (ft)
    (3) Far Point (ft)
  c. Straight Stream:
	300
	
	$\leq$ Within 30 feet of front bumper
	
	$\geq$ 30
	$\geq$ 50
	Range at least 150 feet
		300
		
		$\geq$ 30
		$\geq$ 50

7. Water Tank: Minimum Rate Capacity (gal)
 	
Percent Deliverable:
 	
  a. On level
  b. On 20% side slope
  c. On 30% ascending/descending grade
	1,500
	
	100%
	75%
	75%
		3,000
		and above
		
		100%
		75%
		75%

8. Dry Chemical Turret Discharge:
  a. Flow Rate:
  b. Range, Far Point:
  c. Width:
	$\geq$ 16 lbs per second
	$\geq$ 100 ft
	$\geq$ 17 ft	

Table 3M. Extinguishing Agent System Performance Standards (Metric).

AGENT SYSTEM PERFORMANCE PARAMETER	VEHICLE CLASS	
	1	2

1. Dry Chemical Handline:
   a. Discharge Rate
   b. Range
	$\geq$ 2.35 kg per sec $\leq$ 3.3 kg per sec
	At least 7.5 m	

2. Clean Agent or Approved Equivalent Handline:
   a. Discharge Rate
   b. Range
	$\geq$ 2.3 kg per sec $\leq$ 3.3 kg per sec
	At least 7.5 m	

3. Reeled Water/Foam Handline:
   a. Nozzle Flow Rate: $\pm$ 5%
   b. Straight Stream Pattern
   c. Dispersed Stream Pattern
	$\geq$ 227 Lpm
	$\geq$ 15 m reach
	$\geq$ 6 m reach and $\geq$ 4.6 m wide	

4. Woven Jacket Water/Foam Handline:
   a. Nozzle Flow Rate: $\pm$ 5%
   b. Straight Stream Pattern
   c. Dispersed Stream Pattern
	$\geq$ 474 Lpm
	$\geq$ 19.5 m reach
	$\geq$ 6 m reach and $\geq$ 4.6 m wide	

5. Primary Turret Discharge:
   a. Flow Rate: (Lpm), (-0%, +10%)
   b. Stream Pattern/Distances:
     (1) Straight/Far Point (m)
     (2) Dispersed/Far Point (m)
     (3) Dispersed/Width (m)
	2,839
	
	58
	19.5
	10.5
		4,542
		
		75
		22.5
		10.5

6. Secondary Turret:
   a. Flow Rate: (Lpm), (-0%, +10%)
   b. Flat Patter Distances:
     (1) Near Point
	1,135
	
	$\leq$ Within 9 meters of front bumper
		1,135

(2) Width (m) (3) Far Point (m)	$\geq$ 9 $\geq$ 15	$\geq$ 9 $\geq$ 15
c. Straight Stream:	Range at least 45 meters	
7. Water Tank: Minimum Rated Capacity (liters) Percent Deliverable:	5,678	11,355 and above

a. On level
   b. On 20% side slope
   c. On 30% ascending/descending grade
	100%
	75%
	75%
		100%
		75%
		75%

8. Dry Chemical Turret Discharge:
   a. Flow Rate:
   b. Range, Far Point:
   c. Width:
	$\geq$ 7 kg. per second
	$\geq$ 30 meters
	$\geq$ 5 meters	

Table 3A. Extinguishing Agent Performance Standards
(High-Reach Extendable Turret–Option).

AGENT SYSTEM PERFORMANCE PARAMETER	VEHICLE CLASS	
	1	2
1. Piercing nozzle: a. Discharge Rate: ±5% b. Dispersed Stream Pattern	≥250 gpm ≥15 ft reach and ≥20 ft wide	

2. Turret Discharge (Bed Position):
a. High Flow Rate: (gpm), (-0%, +10%)
b. Stream Pattern/Distances:
   (1) Straight/Far Point (ft)
   (2) Dispersed/Far Point (ft)
   (3) Dispersed/Width (ft)
	750
	
	190
	65
	35
		1,000
		
		230
		70
		35

3. Turret Discharge (Bed Position):
a. Low Flow Rate: (gpm), (-0%, +10%)
b. Stream Pattern/Distances:
   (1) Straight/Far Point (ft)
   (2) Dispersed/Far Point (ft)
   (3) Dispersed/Width (ft)
	375
	
	≥160
	60
	35
		500
		
		≥160
		60
		35

4. Dry Chemical Turret Discharge:
  a. Flow Rate:
  b. *Range, Far Point:
  c. Width:
	≥12 lbs per second
	≥100 ft
	≥17 ft	

5. Clean Agent or Approved Equivalent Turret Discharge:
 	
  a. Flow Rate:
  b. **Range:
	≥7 lbs per second
	At least 25 ft	

*__NOTE:__ Nozzles that entrain or capture dry chemical into the agent master stream may comply with the Far Point Range while simultaneously discharging water/foam agent.

**__NOTE:__ If the piercing nozzle is also used as the Clean Agent nozzle, the discharge pattern is fully dispersed and the 25-foot range is not applicable.

Table 4. Foam Quality Standards.

Foam Concentrate Type (1) Foam Concentrate Type (1) (2)						
Protein and Fluoroprotein Air-Aspirated			Aqueous Film-Forming Foam and Film-Forming Fluoroprotein Foam			
			Air-Aspirated		Nonaspirated	
	Expansion Ratio (range)	Minimum 25% Drain Time (minutes)	Minimum Expansion Ratio	Minimum 25% Drain Time (minutes)	Minimum Expansion Ratio	Minimum 25% Drain Time (minutes)
Handlines	8-12	5	5	4	3	1
Turrets	8-12	5	5	4	3	1

(1)   *The foams used to test the vehicle foam system performance are assumed to meet the industry standards for acceptable aircraft fire fighting foams. For example, the non-film-forming foam (e.g., protein/fluoroprotein foam) must be capable of passing Underwriters Standard UL-162 (Type 3 Application) and the film-forming foams must be capable of passing at least the 50 square-feet fire extinguishment test and the burnback resistance test of MIL-F-24385.*

(2)   *Foams that are labeled as "universal," "multi-purpose," "polar solvent," "3%/6%," or "alcohol foams" should not be used in an airport ARFF vehicle unless the ARFF vehicle is specifically designed with a proportioning system, a foam storage tank, and piping intended for use with this type of agent.*

CHAPTER 4. QUALITY ASSURANCE.

Section 1. General Consideration.

100. CRITERIA FOR VEHICLE ACCEPTANCE. Compliance with this guide specification shall be documented by one more of the following methods:

a. Manufacturer's Certification.

(1) The ARFF vehicle manufacturer shall comply with this requirement by providing a signed component manufacturer's application approval for the specific components listed in Paragraph 103. The signed application approvals or a clear copy of the original shall be made part of the vehicle documentation package.

(2) The ARFF vehicle manufacturer shall provide a written certification that the specific subsystems listed in Paragraph 104 comply with the applicable performance, design, or construction requirements of this guide specification. A signed copy of the certification shall be made part of the vehicle documentation.

b. Prototype Vehicle Tests.

(1) The manufacturer shall conduct the tests specified in Paragraph 105 on the "first article" (i.e., prototype vehicle) produced to meet the performance criteria of this guide specification. A mutually acceptable third party (independent testing agency/laboratory/service) must conduct the required tests or witness the tests that are carried out by the manufacturer. This third party shall record and sign the results of these tests.

(2) A copy of the signed test report(s) shall be made part of the vehicle documentation package. These tests need not be repeated for follow-on production vehicles. However, if substantive changes in design are made or unusual options are requested that could reasonably be expected to affect one or more of the required vehicle performance criteria, such as weight distribution and center of gravity change, the applicable test shall be repeated.

c. Production Vehicle Acceptance Tests.

(1) The ARFF vehicle manufacturer shall conduct the tests listed in Paragraph 121 on every production vehicle. These tests may be conducted at the manufacturer's facility, the airport, or another mutually acceptable test site.

(2) The test managers shall record and sign the results of these tests. A copy of the signed test report(s) shall be made part of each production vehicle documentation package.

101. TECHNICAL SERVICE, PERFORMANCE DOCUMENTATION, AND TRAINING.

a. The vehicle documentation package shall include two copies each of the Operator's Manual, the Parts Manual, and the Maintenance/Service Manual applicable to the specific vehicle. It shall also include one signed copy of each of the certification(s) and test report(s) required by Paragraph 100.a, b, and c.

(1) The Operator's Manual shall include all information required for the safe and efficient operation of the automotive chassis, the fire extinguishing equipment, and any special attachments or auxiliary equipment. The manual shall illustrate and describe the location and function of all controls and instruments. The manual shall at least—

(a) Cover preparation of the vehicle for service upon receipt from the manufacturer.

(b) Give a general description of, and step-by-step instructions for, the operation of the vehicle and its fire extinguishing system(s).

(c) Provide checklists for the daily maintenance inspections and mission readiness checks that the operator is expected to perform.

(d) Provide schedules for required preventative maintenance and required periodic maintenance.

(2) The Parts Manual shall include illustrations and expanded views, as needed, to properly identify all parts, assemblies, subassemblies, and special equipment. All components of assemblies shown in illustrations or expanded views shall be identified by reference numbers that correspond to the reference numbers in the parts lists. All purchased parts shall be cross-referenced with the original manufacturer's name and part number. The parts list shall indicate the quantity of each item used per vehicle. The manual shall contain an alphabetical and a numerical parts list in addition to a table of contents.

(3) The Maintenance/Service Manual shall identify any special tools and test equipment required and shall cover troubleshooting and maintenance as well as minor and major repair procedures. The text shall contain performance specifications, tolerances, and fluid capacities; current, voltage, and resistance data; hydraulic, pneumatic, and electrical diagrams; and such other illustrations and expanded views as may be required to permit proper maintenance by qualified mechanics. The manual shall also contain an alphabetical subject index as well as a table of contents.

(4) The Certification Documents and Test Reports shall be bound or otherwise packaged in a manner suitable for filing.

b. Upon delivery to the airport, the manufacturer shall, at no additional cost, provide the services of a qualified technician for a period of 5 working days to provide thorough instruction in the use, operation, and maintenance of the vehicle. This setup shall include operator training for the primary operators, which will give them sufficient knowledge to train other personnel in the functional use of all fire fighting and vehicle operating systems. The technician should also provide initial adjustments to the vehicle for operational readiness and mount any ancillary appliances included as part of the vehicle that were not factory installed. Prior to leaving the vehicle, the technician should review the maintenance instructions with the purchaser's mechanical personnel to acquaint them with maintenance procedures as well as how to obtain support service for the vehicle. Training shall include written operating instructions that depict the step-by-step operational use of the vehicle. Written instructions shall include, or be supplemented with, materials that can be used to train subsequent new operators.

102. NAMEPLATES AND INSTRUCTION PLATES.

a. All nameplates and instruction plates shall be made of material that will not degrade from weathering or exposure to water, fire fighting agents, vehicle operating fluids, or hydrocarbon fuels and solvents. The information may be engraved, stamped, or etched on the plate. All plates shall be attached with screws, bolts, or rivets, as appropriate for the location. Each plate shall be mounted in a conspicuous place on or near the item it identifies or for which it gives instructions.

b. Nameplates shall show make, model, serial number, and other such data as may be appropriate for positive item identification.

c. Instruction plates shall provide specific directions to be followed for safe, efficient operation or servicing of the vehicle or equipment. These plates shall include specific warnings or cautions necessary to protect operation and maintenance personnel from such hazards as high voltage, pressure and temperature, sharp edges, moving parts, or hazardous materials. These plates shall be so located and of sufficient size to be readily seen under normal operating and service conditions. Instruction plates essential to the safe and effective operation of the vehicle and fire suppression system(s) shall be illuminated for night operations. For example, there shall be a data plate visible to the driver that includes vehicle weights and dimensions and the manufacturer's safe dynamic side slope operation. Another data plate should list all fluid types and capacities for the intended use.

Section 2. Certification of Performance.

103. COMPONENT MANUFACTURER'S CERTIFICATION. The vehicle manufacturer shall provide a copy of the component manufacturer's certification (signed application approval) for each of the following ARFF vehicle components:

a. Axles.

b. Complementary Agent Pressure Relief Device.

c. Complementary Agent Storage Container.

d. Engine(s); Prime Mover(s) and Pump, if separate

e. Handline Hose(s) with Couplings Attached.

f. Propellant Gas Cylinder(s).

g. Propellant Gas Cylinder Regulating Device.

h. Tires.

i. Transfer Case.

j. Transmission.

k. Wheels.

104. VEHICLE MANUFACTURER'S CERTIFICATION. The vehicle manufacturer shall certify in writing that the following components or subsystems comply with the applicable requirements of this AC or a comparable, recognized standard:

Component:	Paragraph Number	Table 2 Item No.
a. Brake		
(1) Air Supply	32.a(1) thru (5)	None
(2) Emergency	32.b	11
(3) Parking	32.c	12
(4) Service	32.d (1) and (2)	10
b. Cooling System	44	None
c. Exhaust System	45	None
d. Fuel System	46	None

Section 3. Prototype Vehicle Performance Tests.

105. PROTOTYPE TEST LIST. The manufacturer, an agent of the manufacturer, or an independent agent or agency shall conduct the tests listed below on the "first article" produced to meet the performance criteria of this guide specification or a comparable recognized standard. Should a major modification, such as a new suspension design, or major alteration, such as installation of a high-reach or extendible turret device, be made to the vehicle, tests to certify compliance with Paragraph 114 must be repeated. Each function tested shall use the specific facilities, equipment, test conditions, test procedures, and the pass/fail criteria detailed in Paragraphs 106 through 119 of this section.

Throughout this section, wherever a test requires the vehicle to be fully loaded, water and foam tanks shall be full, and ballast shall be used as needed to account for the crew and equipment allowance. The ballast shall be arranged so as to distribute the weight in a manner that closely simulates the items being represented. The ballast shall not be shaped or distributed in a manner that creates a favorable, artificial center of gravity. Tires shall be inflated to the manufacturer's recommended cold inflation pressure.

a. Brake Systems:

(1) Grade Holding-Service and Parking.

(2) Stop Distance-Service and Emergency.

b. Complementary Agent Systems:

(1) Handline Discharge Rate and Range.

(a) Dry Chemical.

(b) Clean Agent or Approved Equivalent.

(2) Propellant Gas.

(3) Purge and Vent System.

(4) System Pressure Regulation.

c. Electrical Charging System.

d. Flexibility of Body and Chassis.

e. Water/Foam Agent System:

(1) Bumper Turret/Ground Sweep Discharge Rate, Range, and Pattern.

(2) Flush Capability.

(3) Handline with Nozzle Discharge Rate, Range, and Pattern.

(4) Proportioning and Foam Quality.

(5) Pump and Roll Capability.

(6) Pump Total Discharge Capacity.

(7) Roof Turret(s):

(a) Azimuth and Elevation Limits, Control, and Indicator.

(b) Control System Resistance.

(c) Discharge Rate, Range, and Pattern.

(8) Tank(s):

AC 150/5220-10C   2/18/02

(a) Fill–Overflow and Vent Capacity.

(b) Minimum Rated Capacity.

(9) Undertruck Nozzle Pattern.

f. Gradability.

g. Radio Interference Suppression.

h. Siren Output: Direction and Magnitude.

i. Stability:

(1) Static/Side Slope (Tilt Table).

(2) Dynamic.

j. Steering System:

(1) Resistance/Operating Force Requirements.

(2) Wall-to-Wall Turning Diameter.

k. Underbody Clearances.

l. Visibility: Included Angles from Driver's Seat.

m. Vehicle Interior Noise Levels.

106. BRAKE SYSTEMS PERFORMANCE.

a.   Facilities.

(1) Tests 1 and 2 require two ramps or inclines (manmade or natural) known to be 20-percent and 50-percent grades.

(2) Tests 3 and 4 may be conducted on any paved surface that can support the vehicle weight and the resulting braking forces and is long enough to allow for the combined acceleration, constant speed, and safe braking distance. The site shall be marked out in a lane that is the width of the vehicle to be tested, plus 4 feet (1.2 m).

(3) A runway or taxiway with a marked center line that meets the length, strength, and other conditions specified is an acceptable alternative test site.

b.   Equipment.

(1) Tests 3 and 4 require a calibrated fifth wheel connected to a ground speed readout device that is accurate to ±0.5 percent of the actual measured speed.

(2) Tests 3 and 4 require a brake-triggered device that will mark the strip recorder to show initial brake application.

(3) Tests 3 and 4 require a strip recorder with sufficient resolution to record the vehicle speed, brake application point, and stop point with the same accuracy as that required for the fifth wheel.

NOTE: The use of other data collecting/recording devices of equal accuracy and precision is acceptable.

(4) A test report notebook or similar record form to be used as a test report worksheet and incorporated into the documentation package for the specific vehicle.

c.   Test Conditions.

(1) The grades used for Tests 1 and 2 shall be dry, smooth, free of loose material, and long enough to accommodate the length and weight of the fully loaded vehicle.

(2) The vehicle shall be fully loaded.

(3) The brakes shall be burnished and adjusted to the manufacturer's specifications.

(4) The surface of the site for Tests 3 and 4 shall be level, dry, smooth, and free of any loose material.

d.   Test Procedures.

(1)   TEST   1.   GradeHolding–Parking Brake.

(a) Drive the vehicle in the forward direction up the 20-percent grade, stop the vehicle using the service brake, and set the parking brake.

(b) Shift the transmission to neutral, release the service brake, and visually monitor the vehicle for 5 minutes for any perceptible wheel rotation. Record the results.

(c) Repeat steps (a) and (b) while backing the vehicle up the grade.

(2)   TEST   2.   Grade Holding–Service Brake.

(a) Drive the vehicle in the forward direction up the 50-percent grade, and stop the vehicle using the service brake.

36

(b) Continue holding the vehicle with the service brake, shift the transmission into neutral, and monitor the vehicle visually for 5 minutes for any perceptible wheel rotation. Record the results.

(c) Repeat steps (a) and (b) while backing the vehicle up the grade.

(3) <u>TEST 3</u>. **Stop Distance–Service Brake.**

(a) Start the vehicle, turn on the strip recorder, accelerate to 20 mph (32 km/h), and maintain that speed for at least 50 feet (15 m).

(b) Apply the service brake as if in a panic stop; hold the brake on until the vehicle stops. Record the printout of the distance traveled from the initial braking until the vehicle came to a stop. Make no steering corrections for vehicle drift during the stop.

(c) Measure and record the perpendicular distance from the nearest lane edge line to the outer most edge of the vehicle's width. Report the measurement as a negative number if the vehicle is outside of the test lane, or

(d) If the test lane has a marked center-line, measure and record the perpendicular distance from the centerline to the outer most edge of the vehicle that is farthest from the centerline of the test lane.

(e) Repeat steps (a) through (d) for two complete cycles in each direction of the test lane; record each braking distance.

(f) Repeat steps (a) through (e) above using a test speed of 40 mph (64 km/h).

(4) <u>TEST 4</u>. **Stop Distance–Emergency Brake.** Repeat Test 3, steps (a) through (e) above, for the emergency brake using only the 40 mph (64 km/h) test speed.

(5) <u>TEST 5</u>. **Circuit Failure–Service Brake.**

(a) Disable one dual brake circuit, and repeat Test 3, steps (a) through (e), for the service brake at a speed of 40 mph (64 km/h).

(b) Reconnect the first circuit, disconnect the second, and repeat Test 3, steps (a) through (e), on the second service brake circuit at 40 mph (64 km/h).

e. **Pass/Fail Criteria.**

(1) The service and parking brake grade holding performance shall comply with the applicable portions of Paragraph 32 and the applicable standards of Table 2, Performance Parameters 10 and 12.

(2) For all stop tests conducted in a lane with outer boundary markers, no portion of the vehicle shall be outside those boundaries after the vehicle stops.

(3) For all stop tests conducted in a lane with a marked centerline, the measured distance from the outer most portion of the vehicle to the centerline of the lane shall be less than one-half of the vehicle width, plus 2 feet (0.6 m).

(4) Each of the four recorded stop distances for the service and emergency brakes shall meet the applicable stopping distance standards of Table 2, Performance Parameters 10 and 11.

(5) For the split circuit service brake test, each of the four recorded stop distances, for each circuit, shall meet the applicable stopping distance standards of Table 2, Performance Parameters 11.

107. COMPLEMENTARY AGENT SYSTEM.

NOTE: If the vehicle manufacturer provides signed test data that verifies system performance; a performance certificate from a third party for a complementary agent system of the same brand, general size, and flow rate; or similar documentation from the complementary agent system manufacturer, that documentation may be submitted as an additional item under the terms of Paragraphs 100 and 103, and the test requirements of this paragraph (but not the pass/fail criteria) shall be waived.

a. **Facilities for Agent System Test Series.** Tests 1, 2, and 3 require a level, open site (free of obstructions within the expected agent range) that is suitable for the discharge of approximately 500 pounds (230 kg) of the complementary agent being tested.

b. **Equipment for the Complementary Agent System Test Series.**

(1) Tests 1, 2, and 3 require a means of removing the agent tank from the vehicle without loss of agent and moving it to the weighing device.

NOTE: Alternatively, the system may be tested as a unit outside the vehicle providing that the agent tank and related piping, fittings, valves, hose, and nozzle(s) are in the same configuration as they will be in when installed on the vehicle. The system may also be tested as an integral part of the completed prototype vehicle as long as the weighing device meets the requirements of Paragraph 107.b(2).

(2) A calibrated scale or load cell with an accuracy of ± 1 percent of the amount of agent to be weighed.

(3) A stopwatch that can be read to ± 0.5 seconds.

(4) A tape measure or other distance measuring device that can be read to ± 0.5 inches.

(5) An anemometer capable of reading wind velocities in the range of 0 to 10 mph (0 to 16 km/h) with ± 0.5 mph (0.8 km/h) accuracy.

(6) Test 4 requires a means of connecting a pressure gauge or transducer between the low-pressure (downstream) side of the regulator and the agent tank inlet valve.

(7) Test 4 requires a calibrated pressure sensing device capable of reading pressure with an accuracy of ± 1 percent of the pressure to be measured.

(8) Test 4 requires a pressure reading device connected to the piping between the low-pressure propellant gas inlet valve and the agent tank top. If the tank is equipped with a gauge having sufficient accuracy, the tank gauge may be used.

(9) A test report notebook or similar record form to be used as a test report worksheet and incorporated into the documentation package.

c.   Test Conditions for Agent System Series.

(1) The complementary agent tank pressure relief device shall have been certified as required in Paragraph 103.b and shall be operational.

(2) The agent tank shall have been certified as required in Paragraph 103.c and shall be clean, dry, and empty.

(3) Propellant gas tanks shall have been certified as required in Paragraph 103.f and shall be pressurized to the recommended operating pressure.

(4) Wind conditions shall be in the range of 0 to 5 mph (0 to 10 km/h).

(5) The vehicle (or alternative test unit) shall have all agent piping operational.

d.   Test Procedures.

(1) TEST 1. Handline Discharge Rate and Range.

NOTE: This test may be combined with Test 4 if sufficient agent remains in the tank.

(a) Charge the agent tank using the manufacturer's recommended agent and fill procedure. Weigh it and record the gross filled weight.

(b) Reconnect the tank to the system and ensure that fill cap(s) are secure, propellant gas lines are connected, discharge nozzles are in the closed position, and all fittings and connections are tight.

(c) Pull all handline hose from the reel(s), and position nozzles so they may be discharged onto the test site without stream obstructions and such that the stream patterns will not overlap. Pressurize the system using the manufacturer's recommended procedure.

(d) Select one of the handline nozzles and hold it in a fixed, horizontal position between 36 and 60 inches (90 and 150 cm) above the ground level. Simultaneously start the stopwatch and fully open the nozzle.

(e) Monitor the time. After approximately 20 seconds of discharge time have elapsed, simultaneously shut down the nozzle and stop the stopwatch.

(f) Measure the level ground distance from the spot directly below the nozzle to the far edge of the discharge pattern. Record this distance as the range for nozzle number one.

(g) Reweigh the dry chemical agent tank, and record this weight as the discharge weight for nozzle number one.

(h) Reconnect the agent tank, pressurize the system, and if there is more than one dry chemical handline, repeat steps (d) through (g) for nozzle number two.

(i) After testing nozzle number two, reconnect the agent tank, pressurize the system, and repeat steps (d) through (g) while simultaneously discharging both handline nozzles.

(j) Calculate the nozzle discharge rates (DRs), in pounds per second, as follows:

Nozzle #1: DR = $\dfrac{\text{Gross Filled Wt - Discharge Wt}}{\text{\#1} \square \text{Time (Seconds)}}$

Nozzle #2: DR = $\dfrac{\text{Discharge Wt \#1 - Discharge Wt}}{\text{\#2} \square \text{Time (Seconds)}}$

Dual Noz: DR = $\dfrac{\text{Discharge Wt \#2 - Discharge Wt Dual}}{2 \times \text{Time (Seconds)}}$

(2) TEST 2. Propellant Gas Quantity.

NOTE: May be combined with Test 3.

(a) Weigh the empty agent tank(s), and record the tare weight.

(b) Charge the agent tank using the manufacturer's recommended agent and fill procedure. Weigh the tank, and record it as the "gross filled weight."

(c) Reconnect the tank to the system and ensure that fill cap(s) are secure, propellant gas lines are connected, discharge nozzles are in the closed position, and all fittings and connections are tight.

(d) Pull all handline hose from the reel(s), and position nozzles so they may be discharged onto the test site with no stream obstructions. Pressurize the system using the manufacturer's recommended procedure.

(e) Simultaneously open all discharge nozzles fully, and continue agent discharge until only the pressurizing gas is discharged. Shut down the propellant gas supply.

(f) Reweigh the agent tank, and record the new weight as the post discharge weight.

(g) Calculate the amount of agent remaining, and report the results, as follows:

$\dfrac{\text{\% Agent}}{\text{Remaining}} = \dfrac{\text{Post Discharge Wt - Tare Wt (x 100)} \square}{\text{Gross Filled Wt - Tare Wt}}$

(3) TEST 3. System Pressure Regulation.

NOTE: May be combined with Test 2.

(a) Charge the agent tank using the manufacturer's recommended agent and fill procedure.

(b) Reconnect the tank to the system, and ensure that fill cap(s) are secure, propellant gas lines are connected, discharge nozzles are in the closed position, and all fittings and connections are tight.

(c) Pull all handline hose from the reel(s), and position nozzles so they may be discharged onto the test site with no stream obstructions. Pressurize the system to the manufacturer's recommended operating pressure using the manufacturer's recommended procedure, and record the agent tank operating pressure.

(d) Simultaneously open fully all discharge nozzles. Continue agent discharge, and monitor and record agent tank pressure at 5-second intervals until only the pressurizing gas is discharged. As soon as only propellant gas is being discharged from all nozzles, shut down the propellant gas supply.

(4) TEST 4. Purge and Vent System.

NOTE: May be combined with Test 1.

(a) Charge the agent tank using the manufacturer's recommended agent and fill procedure.

(b) Reconnect the tank to the system, and ensure that fill cap(s) are secure, propellant gas lines are connected, discharge nozzles are in the closed position, and all fittings and connections are tight.

(c) Pull all handline hose from the reel(s), and position nozzles so they may be discharged onto the test site with no stream obstructions. Pressurize the system to the manufacturer's recommended operating pressure using the manufacturer's recommended procedure, and record the agent tank operating pressure.

(d) Simultaneously open fully all discharge nozzles. Continue agent discharge for approximately 10 seconds, and then shut down all nozzles.

(e) Purge all discharge lines and nozzles using the manufacturer's recommended procedure.

(f) Vent the agent tank using the manufacturer's recommended procedure.

e. Pass/Fail Criteria.

(1) The discharge rate from each nozzle shall fall within the standard range specified in Table 3, Performance Parameter 1.a or 2.a, and shall be within ± 10 percent of each other.

(2) The range from each nozzle shall meet or exceed the standard specified in Table 3, Performance Parameter 1.b or 2.b.

(3) When discharged simultaneously, the averaged discharge rate from either nozzle shall be within ± 10 percent of either nozzle discharging alone.

(4) There shall be sufficient propellant gas remaining after agent discharge stops to purge all agent lines clear of agent from the tank through, and including, the hose line(s) and nozzle(s).

(5) The amount of agent remaining in the tank(s) after agent discharge stops shall not exceed 5 percent of the initial quantity.

(6) The performance of the pressure regulating device shall be acceptable if it is capable of maintaining the tank pressure within the manufacturer's recommended operating pressure range throughout the entire discharge time.

(7) At the end of the purge process (for a dry chemical system), loose agent shall not be left lying in the horizontal piping beyond the agent tank valve.

(8) The depressurization/venting process shall allow only minimal quantities (i.e., 1 pound (0.5 kg) or less) of the agent to escape from the agent tank.

(9) The venting process shall NOT allow any agent to enter the discharge piping, handlines, or nozzles.

108. ELECTRICAL CHARGING SYSTEM.

a. Facilities. This test requires an area suitable for running the engine(s) while the electrical loads are operating and the charging current and voltages are being measured.

b. Equipment Required.

(1) The vehicle tachometer, as installed.

(2) A voltmeter with a range compatible with the design voltage of the vehicle electrical system and that can be read with an accuracy of ± 0.1 volt.

(3) Two ammeters, with a range compatible with the current load, that can be read within ± 1 percent of the actual current flow.

(4) A test report notebook or similar record form to be used as a test report worksheet and incorporated into the documentation package.

c. Test Conditions.

(1) Ensure the batteries are fully charged; i.e., the specific gravity of each battery shall be at the manufacturer's specifications.

(2) Ensure the vehicle electrical system and charging device are fully operational.

(3) The ambient temperature shall be within the range of 50° to 90° F (10° to 32° C).

(4) Install the voltmeter to continuously measure the battery voltage.

(5) Install an ammeter in a manner that will permit reading of the current flow from the battery to the electrical devices.

(6) Install a second ammeter in a manner that will permit reading the maximum current flow from the alternator to the rest of the electrical system, excluding the starter.

(7) Start the engine and allow it to run, with all electrical devices turned off, long enough to recharge the batteries prior to beginning the test.

d. Test Procedure. Voltage and current flow readings shall be recorded for the following conditions:

(1) Engine at idle with—

(a) Battery alone.

(b) All electrical devices normally expected to be operating simultaneously turned on.

(2) Engine at 50 percent of governed speed with all electrical devices normally expected to be operating simultaneously turned on.

(3) Engine at maximum governed speed with all electrical devices normally expected to be operating simultaneously turned on.

e. Pass/Fail Criteria. The electrical system performance shall be acceptable if it meets or exceeds the following:

(1) Engine at idle with—

(a) Battery alone.

(i) Voltage at the battery shall remain above 13 volts.

(ii) Current output shall equal the battery manufacturer's recommended charging rate if less than 50 amps or be at least 50 amps while the battery is charging.

(b) All electrical devices normally expected to be operating simultaneously turned on.

(i) Voltage at the battery shall remain above 13 volts.

(ii) Current output shall be at least 50 amps or shall be equal to the sum of the current demand of the operating electrical devices if that current demand is lower than 50 amps.

(2) Engine at 50 percent of governed speed with all electrical devices normally expected to be operating simultaneously turned on.

(a) Voltage at the battery shall remain above 13 volts.

(b) Current output shall be equal to the sum of the current demand of the operating electrical devices.

(3) Engine at maximum governed speed with all electrical devices normally expected to be operating simultaneously turned on.

(a) Voltage at battery shall remain above 13 volts.

(b) Current output shall be equal to the sum of the current demand of the operating electrical devices.

109. BODY AND CHASSIS FLEXIBILITY.

a. **Facilities.** This test requires a flat area suitable for discharging agent and driving the vehicle onto portable ramps.

b. **Equipment Required.**

(1) Two to four double-ended ramps with a flat top long enough for the whole tire footprint. The approach and departure slopes of the ramps shall be graded to allow the vehicle to ascend and descend safely. The height of the ramps shall be 14 inches.

(2) A test report notebook or similar record form to be used as a test report worksheet and incorporated into the documentation package.

c. **Test Conditions.** The vehicle shall be tested in its fully loaded condition.

d. **Test Procedure.**

(1) <u>TEST 1.</u> **4 x 4 Vehicles.**

(a) Drive the vehicle onto two ramps positioned to raise the diagonally opposite front and rear wheels.

(b) Inspect the vehicle for any visible signs of clearance between the tires and the ground or supporting ramp surfaces, component interference, sheet metal buckling, and interference with moving parts, including doors and equipment compartment closures. Record the results.

(c) Demonstrate the operation of all electrical, pneumatic, hydraulic, and agent systems, including the discharge of agent from all orifices. Record the results.

(d) Drive the vehicle off the ramps, and reposition them to raise the other two diagonally opposite front and rear wheels.

(e) Repeat steps (b) and (c) above.

(f) Review the test record for any misfits or malfunctions, make any necessary repairs, and repeat the test as necessary.

(2) <u>TEST 2.</u> **6 x 6 Vehicles.**

(a) Drive the vehicle onto two ramps positioned to raise a front wheel and the diagonally opposite rear wheel on axle number three.

(b) Repeat steps (b) and (c) in Test 1 above.

(c) Drive the vehicle off the ramps, position a third ramp so the second rear wheel on the same side will also be elevated, and repeat steps (b) and (c) in Test 1 above.

(d) Reposition the vehicle/ramps so as to raise the other set of wheels and repeat steps (a) through (c) above.

(e) Review the test record for any misfits or malfunctions, make any necessary repairs, and repeat the test as necessary.

(3) TEST 3. 8 x 8 Vehicles.

(a) Drive the vehicle onto two ramps positioned to raise the front wheel on axle number one and the diagonally opposite rear wheel on axle number four.

(b) Repeat steps (b) and (c) in Test 1 above.

(c) Drive the vehicle off the ramps, position two additional ramps so the second front and rear wheels on the same side will also be elevated, and repeat steps (b) and (c) in Test 1 above.

(d) Reposition the vehicle and ramps so as to raise the other set of wheels, and repeat the test.

(e) Review the test record for any misfits or malfunctions, make any necessary repairs, and repeat the test as necessary.

e. Pass/Fail Criteria.

(1) There shall be no interference between one moving part and any other part or between any moving part and an adjacent surface, structural member, or mounting device.

(2) All doors, equipment compartment closures, and hose reels shall function normally.

(3) There shall be no loss of performance in any operating subsystem.

(4) If there is any contact introduced by the twisting motion of the vehicle frame between major components (e.g., cab, agent tanks, engine compartment(s); engines, pumps, hose reels, and the respective compartment walls and mounting fixtures; etc.) that contact shall not damage or exhibit the potential to damage either component during the repeated flexing that is expected in normal service.

(5) There shall be no visible signs of clearance between any vehicle tire and the ground or ramp surfaces.

110. WATER/FOAM AGENT SYSTEM.

a. Facilities.

(1) A number of tests in this series require a paved open area suitable for discharging large volumes of water/foam solution at high pressure. In Test 14, the area must have sufficient strength and size to accommodate the safe maneuvering of a fully loaded

vehicle at speeds up to 25 mph (40 km/h). In Test 1, the area must include measured grades of 20 and 30 percent.

(2) An off-road area with similar characteristics to accommodate the safe maneuvering of a fully loaded vehicle at speeds up to 10 mph (16 km/h) is also required for Test 15.

(3) In addition, a site suitable for discharging agent that includes a grade of 40 percent and that is at least twice the length of the vehicle being tested is required for Test 16. If the alternate draw bar method is used, Test 16A requires a level, paved test pad adequate for an extended draw bar pull that is also suitable for the discharge of large volumes of agent at high pressure.

(4) All tests require a water supply sufficient to refill vehicle tank(s), as needed.

(5) Test 1 requires a means of delivering water to the tank inlet at 80 psi (5.5 Bar) and in sufficient volume to permit the filling of the tank of the appropriate vehicle class in 2 minutes or less.

b. Equipment required.

(1) As required to perform specific tests in this series in accordance with NFPA 412, Standard for Evaluating Foam Fire Fighting Equipment on Aircraft Rescue and Fire Fighting Vehicles.

(2) Vehicle/pump engine(s) speedometer, tachometer, and agent system discharge pressure gauge, as installed by the manufacturer.

(3) A stopwatch that can be read to ± 0.5 seconds.

(4) A supply of foam concentrate sufficient to refill the vehicle foam tank(s), as needed.

(5) Test 1 requires two water pressure measuring devices with an accuracy of ± 1 percent of the pressure being measured, calibrated sight gauges, and a liquid volume measuring device with an accuracy of ± 1 percent of the volume being measured.

(6) Tests 3, 4, 14, 15, 16, and 16A require a supply of an approved water-soluble dye.

(7) If one of the optional flow rate methods described in Tests 5A, 7A, or 11A is used, a calibrated sight gauge, a calibrated open top receiver of sufficient capacity to collect at least 25 percent of the water tank

volume, or appropriate flow meters capable of being read to ± 1 percent of the liquid volume to be measured will be needed.

(8) Tests 9, 10, and 11 require a tape measure capable of measuring 30 feet (9 m) with an accuracy of ± 0.5 inches (1.25 cm), a 3-foot (1 m) carpenter's level, a large protractor with an accuracy of ± 1 degree, and a spring scale or other suitable measuring device that can be attached to the turret or turret control handle and has an accuracy of ± 1 percent of the quantity being measured.

(9) Test 13 requires a means of marking or defining the vehicle plan view on the ground and for marking the undertruck nozzle discharge pattern on the plan view outline.

(10) If the alternate draw bar pull method is used in Test 16A, a load cell, accurate to within ± 500 pounds (230 kg), and a variable load dynamometer sled are required.

(11) A test report notebook or similar record form to be used as a test report worksheet and incorporated into the documentation package is required.

c. **Test Conditions.**

(1) Verify and record the fact that the agent system pressure relief valve has been set to the recommended relief pressure and is functioning prior to the beginning of any test in this series.

(2) To ensure test operator safety and to validate the effectiveness of subsystem integration, perform and pass this series of tests in the order presented.

(3) Make sure the temperature of the water and the foam concentrate are within the foam manufacturer's recommended operating temperature range.

(4) Ensure the water and foam tanks are full at the start and refilled as needed to complete the tests.

(5) Set the foam concentrate proportioners at the appropriate rate for the foam concentrate to be used at the airport.

(6) Set the agent selector for water/foam discharge.

(7) Ensure the vehicle is fully loaded.

(8) The engine(s) and transmission shall be at a normal operating temperature.

(9) Handlines shall be fully deployed and the nozzles shall be set for straight stream during discharge rate tests.

(10) Ensure the agent pump, fill system, overflow/vent system, water and foam discharge system, foam proportioning system, and primary turret(s) are fully operational during these tests.

d. **Test procedures.**

(1) **TEST 1. Fill, Overflow, and Vent.**

(a) At the beginning of this test, ensure the vehicle is parked on level ground, the water tank fill and vent system is fully operational, the water tank(s) are empty, and the pressure measuring devices are attached to the vehicle in such a manner that the internal tank pressure and the tank inlet pressure can be monitored during the tank filling process.

(b) Maintain the water supply pressure at the tank inlet at 80 psi (5.5 Bar) ± 5 percent throughout the filling and overflow process.

(c) Simultaneously initiate flow to the tank and start the stopwatch. Stop and record the time at the first flow of water from the overflow vent.

(d) Continue the flow of water while maintaining 80 psi (5.5 Bar) at the tank inlet and continue to monitor the tank pressure for an additional 30 seconds. Shut off the water, and record the highest pressure reached during the overflow period.

(2) **TEST 2. Minimum Rated Capacity.**

(a) With the vehicle parked on level ground and sight gauges attached to both the water and foam concentrate tanks, fill the inlet piping until the water reaches the bottom of the tanks. Do not record the volume of water used. Add an appropriate quantity of an approved water-soluble dye to the foam concentrate tank.

(b) The tank(s) shall be filled using a liquid volume measuring device. At approximately every 2 percent of the tank capacity for the bottom 25 percent and every 10 percent of the remaining tank capacity, the volume added shall be correlated with the sight gauge(s) calibrations. If necessary, a correction table or graph shall be prepared for each sight gauge on each tank. When the tanks are filled to the top, the total volume of water added to each tank shall be recorded as "Water Tank Full" or "WTF" and "Foam Concentrate Tank Full" or "FCTF."

(c) With the agent system set to discharge foam and tanks completely full, discharge shall be initiated and continued at the maximum turret discharge setting. At the first indication of a discharge pressure drop (pump cavitation), stop agent discharge. Dye shall be visible in the discharge stream throughout the test.

(d) Measure and record the volume of water remaining in each tank as "Water Tank Empty" or "WTE" and "Foam Concentrate Tank–Load # 1" or "FCT-L1."

(e) Calculate and record the difference between the volume of the liquid in the water tank recorded in steps (b) and (d) as the volume of water discharged from that tank on level ground, i.e., "Rated Water Tank Capacity–Level."

(f) Refill only the water tank, and repeat steps (c) through (e) until all usable liquid has been discharged from the foam concentrate tank. Record and measure the volume of water remaining in the foam concentrate tank as "FTC-LX," where X represents the number of loads of water used to deplete the foam tank volume.

(g) Calculate and record the difference between the initial volume (FCTF) recorded in step (b) and the "empty" volume (FCT-LX) from step (f) as the volume of "foam" discharged from that tank on level ground; i.e., the "Rated Foam Tank Capacity–Level."

(h) Refill both tanks, and repeat steps (c) through (g). Record "Rated Water/Foam Tank Capacities" with the vehicle positioned as follows:

(i) 20-percent side slope, left side up slope.

(ii) 20-percent side slope, right side up slope.

(iii) 30-percent ascending grade.

(iv) 30-percent descending grade.

(3) TEST 3. **Flush Capability.**

(a) Fill the water and foam concentrate tanks with water, and add a suitable amount of an approved water-soluble dye to the foam tank.

(b) While operating in the foam mode, discharge agent through each water/foam discharge orifice until dye is detected. After dye is seen in the discharge stream of all orifices, shut off the discharge and record the dyed water volume remaining in the foam concentrate tank.

(c) Change the agent system settings to the flush mode, and discharge water through each water/foam discharge orifice. As soon as the water runs clear from all orifices, shut off the discharge, record the dyed water volume remaining in the foam concentrate tank, and drain the piping.

(4) TEST 4. **Pump Total Discharge Capacity.**

NOTE: If the vehicle is equipped with multiple pumps, they shall be operated in parallel during this test.

(a) Start the vehicle engine(s).

(b) Engage the agent pump(s) and bring them up to pumping pressure with all agent applicator outlets closed. Observe and record pump pressure.

(c) Adjust roof turret elevation to optimum range position, open the roof turret discharge valve, observe the range of turret stream, continue flow to allow system pressure to stabilize, and observe and record discharge pressure.

(d) Continue turret discharge and initiate discharge from each of the following in its turn: the ground sweep or bumper turret, the primary handlines (add one at a time), and the undertruck nozzles. Discharge all applicators simultaneously in a straight stream.

NOTE: As each additional applicator is turned on, the range of the initial turret stream and the initial range of each added appliance stream should be compared by observation. Observe system pressure, and, after system pressure stabilization, record the pressure.

(e) Continue discharging with all applicators flowing until the system pressure has stabilized. Record the pressure and stop the test.

(5) TEST 5. **Bumper Turret or Ground Sweep Discharge Rate.**

NOTE: If the vehicle is equipped with multiple pumps, they shall be operated in parallel during this test.

(a) Start the vehicle engine(s).

(b) Engage the agent pump(s) and bring them up to pumping pressure with all agent applicator outlets closed. Observe and record pump discharge pressure.

(c) Open the discharge valve to full flow position, and start the stopwatch.

(d) Continue discharge, and observe the discharge pressure gauge. At the first sign of pump cavitation (indicated by a significant drop in discharge pressure), stop the stopwatch, and disengage the water pump. Record the time.

(e) Calculate the discharge rate (DR) in gallons per minute, as follows:

$$DR = \frac{\text{Minimum Rated Tank Capacity (Unit Vol)}}{\text{Discharge Time (min)}}$$

(6) **TEST 5A.** **Optional Procedures: Sight Gauge or Flow Meter.**

(a) Steps (a) and (b) of Test 5 apply.

(b) Open the discharge valve to the full flow position, monitor the discharge pressure gauge, and after pressure stabilizes, simultaneously read the initial tank volume (ITV) on the sight gauge and start the stop watch. After at least 1 minute of discharge, simultaneously read the remaining tank volume (RTV) and stop the watch. If a flow meter is used, read and record the flow rates at 15-second intervals during at least 1 minute of discharge.

(c) Report the average of the flow meter readings, or calculate and report the DR from the sight gauge results, as follows:

$$DR = \frac{\text{Initial Tank Vol - Remaining Tank Vol}}{\text{Discharge Time (min)}}$$

(7) **TEST 6.** **Bumper Turret or Ground Sweep Range and Pattern.**

NOTE: This test may be combined with Test 17.

(a) Start the vehicle engine(s).

(b) Engage the agent pump(s) and bring them up to pumping pressure with all agent applicator outlets closed.

(c) The test measurements for range and pattern of the water/foam solution discharge shall be conducted as described in NFPA 412.

(8) **TEST 7.** **Handline Nozzle Discharge Rate.**

NOTE: If the vehicle is equipped with multiple pumps, they shall be operated in parallel during this test.

(a) Adjust the handline nozzle(s) pattern(s) to straight stream position. If the nozzle is nonaspirated, repeat this test or one of the optional tests with the nozzle pattern setting in the fully dispersed position.

(b) Start the vehicle engine(s).

(c) Engage the agent pump(s) and bring them up to pumping pressure with all agent applicator outlets closed. Observe and record pump discharge pressure.

(d) Open the handline nozzle control valve to full flow position, and start the stopwatch.

(e) Continue discharge, and observe the discharge pressure gauge. At the first sign of a significant drop in discharge pressure, stop the watch and disengage the water pump. Record the time.

(f) Calculate the DR, as follows:

$$DR = \frac{\text{Minimum Rated Tank Capacity (Unit Vol)}}{\text{Discharge Time (min)}}$$

(g) Service the vehicle, and repeat steps (a) through (f) for each handline.

(9) **TEST 7A.** **Optional Procedures:** Using sight gauge, calibrated open top receiving tank, or flow meter, repeat steps (a) through (c) of Test 7.

(a) **Sight Gauge.** Open discharge valve to full flow position, monitor the discharge pressure gauge, and after the pressure stabilizes, simultaneously read the ITV on the sight gauge, and start the stopwatch. After approximately 50 percent of the remaining water has been discharged, simultaneously read the RTV and stop the watch. Report the discharge rate based on the sight gauge results, calculated as follows:

$$DR = \frac{\text{Initial Tank Vol - Remaining Tank Vol}}{\text{Discharge Time (min)}}$$

Or

(b) Flow Meter. Open the discharge valve to full flow position, monitor the discharge pressure gauge, and after pressure stabilizes, read and record flow rates at 15-second intervals during discharge of at least 50 percent of the minimum rated tank capacity. Report the discharge rate based on the averaged flow meter readings,

Or

(c) Calibrated Receiver. Open the discharge valve to full flow position, monitor the discharge pressure gauge, and after the pressure stabilizes, simultaneously direct the handline discharge stream into the open top of the calibrated receiver and start the stopwatch. When the receiver is full, stop the stopwatch, and shut down the stream. Repeat the process three times, calculate the results as shown below, and report the average.

$$DR = \frac{\text{Calibrated Receiver Tank Vol}}{\text{Discharge Time (min)}}$$

(10) TEST 8. Handline Nozzle Discharge Range and Pattern.

NOTE: This test may be combined with Test 17.

(a) Start the vehicle engine(s).

(b) Engage the agent pump(s) and bring them up to pumping pressure with all agent applicator outlets closed.

(c) The test measurements for range and pattern of the water/foam solution discharge shall be conducted as described in NFPA 412.

(11) TEST 9. Roof Turret(s) Azimuth and Elevation Limits.

NOTE: If provided, the turret power assist system shall be fully operational during this test.

(a) Point the turret parallel to the vehicle length, and elevate it to the maximum vertical travel. The angle formed by a horizontal, level line through the vertical rotation axis and the turret barrel centerline shall be measured and recorded.

(b) Rotate the turret to its maximum horizontal travel (both left and right of the straight ahead position) when the turret is—

(i) At maximum vertical depression.

(ii) At maximum elevation.

(iii) In the horizontal position.

(c) Measure and record the angle of turret rotation, left and right of center, for each of these configurations.

(d) Place markers or a line perpendicular to the vehicle centerline and 30 feet (9 m) in front of the forward edge of the front bumper. The turret shall be:

(i) Aimed parallel to the vehicle centerline.

(ii) Lowered to its maximum vertical depression.

(iii) Set for maximum dispersed pattern.

(iv) Set to operate at maximum design flow rate.

With the turret at these settings, activate the agent system and discharge water. Note and record the point of impact relative to the line or markers, and measure and record the actual distance.

(12) TEST 10. Roof Turret Control System Resistance.

NOTE: If provided, the turret power assist shall be fully operational and used during the control force measurements.

(a) Attach a suitable spring scale or other measuring device to the turret in such a manner that the forces at the turret control handle can be measured.

(b) Set the turret discharge for a straight stream at maximum flow rate. Measure and record the force required to—

(i) Start turret movement from center to the left and to the right.

(ii) Continue the turret movement, after start from center, to the left and right stops.

(iii) Start turret movement from the full left and right stops.

(iv) Continue the turret movement, after start from both the left and right stops, to the opposite stop.

(v) Start turret movement from horizontal to the elevated and the depressed positions.

(vi) Continue the turret movement, after start from the horizontal, to both the elevated and the depressed stops.

(vii) Start the turret movement from both the elevated and depressed stops.

(viii) Continue the turret movement after start from both the elevated and depressed stops to the opposite stop.

(c) Change the turret discharge to maximum flow with dispersed pattern, and repeat steps (b)(i) through (viii).

(13) TEST 11. Turret Discharge Rate.

NOTE: If the vehicle is equipped with multiple pumps, the pumps shall be operated in parallel during this test.

(a) Adjust the turret to full flow, straight stream pattern, and elevate it to the optimum range position.

(b) Start the vehicle engine(s).

(c) Engage the agent pump(s) and bring them up to pumping pressure with all agent applicator outlets closed. Observe and record pump discharge pressure.

(d) Open turret discharge valve to full flow position, and start the stopwatch.

(e) Continue discharge, and observe the discharge pressure gauge. At the first sign of a significant drop in discharge pressure, stop the watch and disengage the water pump. Record the time.

(f) Calculate the DR, as follows:

$$DR = \frac{Minimum\ Rated\ Tank\ Capacity\ (Unit\ Vol)}{Discharge\ Time\ (min)}$$

(g) Change the turret pattern adjustment to the fully dispersed pattern. Retain the full flow discharge and elevation/optimum range setting. Repeat steps (b) through (g).

(h) If applicable, change the turret flow rate to half flow, and repeat steps (a) through (g).

(14) TEST 11A. Optional Procedures: Sight Gauge or Flow Meter.

(a) Follow steps (a) through (c) in Test 11.

(b) Sight Gauge. Open the discharge valve to full flow position, monitor the discharge pressure gauge, and, after the pressure stabilizes, simultaneously read the ITV on the sight gauge and start the stopwatch. After approximately 50 percent of the remaining water has been discharged, simultaneously read the RTV and stop the stopwatch. Report the DR based on sight gauge results calculated as follows:

$$DR = \frac{Initial\ Tank\ Vol - Remaining\ Tank\ Vol}{Discharge\ Time\ (min)}$$

Or

(c) Flow Meter. Open the discharge valve to full flow position, monitor the discharge pressure gauge, and after the pressure stabilizes, read and record flow rates at 15-second intervals during the discharge of at least 50 percent of the minimum rated tank capacity. Report the discharge rate based on the averaged flow meter readings.

(d) Change the turret pattern to the fully dispersed pattern. Retain the full flow discharge and elevation/optimum range setting. Repeat steps (a) and (b) or (a) and (c).

(e) If applicable, change the turret flow rate to half flow, and repeat steps (a) and (b) or (a) and (c).

(15) TEST 12. Turret Range and Pattern.

NOTE: This test may be combined with Test 17.

(a) Start the vehicle engine(s).

(b) Engage the agent pump(s) and bring them up to pumping pressure with all agent applicator outlets closed.

(c) The test measurements for range and pattern of the turret(s) water/foam solution discharge shall be conducted as described in NFPA 412.

(16) TEST 13. Undertruck Nozzle Pattern.

NOTE: The agent discharge system shall be fully operational during this test.

(a) Set the agent system to operate in the foam mode, and engage the agent pumps with all discharge orifices closed.

(b) As soon as the discharge pressure stabilizes, set the undertruck nozzles to discharge simultaneously and continuously until there is a clearly defined pattern of foam under the vehicle.

(c) Stop the discharge and mark, measure, and record the boundaries of the pattern.

(17) TEST 14. Pump and Roll Capability–Paved Surface.

NOTE: This test may be combined with Test 15.

(a) While operating the vehicle on a paved surface at a speed of approximately 20 mph (30 km/h), engage and disengage the agent system pump(s) for at least three cycles. Record any irregular vehicle or pump performance.

(b) Slow the vehicle to approximately 5 mph (8 km/h), prepare the primary turret(s) and ground sweep or bumper turret to discharge, and initiate agent discharge through the primary turret(s) and the ground sweep/bumper turret.

(c) Maneuver the vehicle forward and backward while discharging and operating at various speeds up to 5 mph (8 km/h). The agent pump(s) shall also be disengaged and engaged for at least three cycles while maneuvering at these speeds. While continuing to maneuver and discharge agent, observe the agent discharge pressure gauge for fluctuations until the water tank is empty. Record agent discharge pressures at 15-second intervals, and note any irregular pump performance.

(18) TEST 15. Pump and Roll–Off-road. The vehicle shall be serviced and moved to a suitable off-road test site. Repeat steps (b) and (c) of Test 14 above.

(19) TEST 16. Pump and Roll–On Grade. The vehicle shall be serviced and moved to a 40 percent grade site.

(a) Position the vehicle at the bottom of the grade, and initiate discharge through the main turret(s) at full rated discharge. Record the stabilized discharge pressure.

(b) Immediately upon stabilization of the discharge pressure, begin ascending the grade until achieving a speed of at least 1 mph (1.6 km/h).

(c) During the ascent, bring the vehicle to a stop and then resume its ascent, regaining a speed of at least 1 mph (1.6 km/h) before ending the test. Record the actual speed achieved and any changes in discharge pressure.

(20) TEST 16A. Pump-and-Roll-Alternate To Test On Grade.

NOTE: If an actual 40-percent grade is not available, the vehicle may be coupled to a "40-percent grade equivalent" draw bar load.

(a) The load cell reading (in unit force per square unit area) required to simulate the 40 percent grade must equal—

$$\frac{\sin 21.8° \text{ x gross vehicle weight}}{\text{square unit area of the load cell}}$$

(b) With the vehicle coupled to the appropriate simulated grade/load, conduct the test as described in Test 16 above.

(21) TEST 17. Proportioning and Foam Quality.

NOTE: This test may be combined with Tests 6, 8, and/or 12.

(a) Start the vehicle engine(s).

(b) Engage the agent pump(s) and bring them up to pumping pressure with all agent applicator outlets closed.

(c) Test the water/foam solution discharged from each of the applicators listed below for foam concentration, expansion ratio, and 25-percent drain time, as described in NFPA 412. Determine and report the foam concentrate delivered by each of the following applicators (while discharging individually and while discharging during combined simultaneous discharge):

(i) Roof turret at full discharge.

(ii) Roof turret at one-half discharge.

(iii) Ground sweep or bumper turret.

(iv) Handline(s) with nozzles provided with truck.

(v) Undertruck nozzles.

e.   Pass/Fail Criteria.

(1) The performance of the water tank inlet system shall be acceptable if the total fill time, when using an inlet water supply with a constant pressure of 80 psi (5.5 Bar) at the tank inlet, is no more than 2 minutes.

(2) The tank vent system shall be acceptable if the internal tank pressure does not exceed the tank manufacturer's recommended operating pressure at any time during the fill or overflow test.

(3) The foam concentrate tank shall be acceptable if it meets or exceeds the requirements of Paragraph 77.

(4) The water tank and the usable capacity shall be acceptable if it meets or exceeds the requirements of Paragraph 80, and the minimum rated capacity conforms to Table 3, Performance Parameters 7.a, b, and c.

(5) The flush system shall not be acceptable if any discharge outlet fails to discharge clear water. Redesign or repair the system, as appropriate, and repeat the test until all discharge orifices discharge clear water.

(6) There shall be no increase (evidence of water tank feedback) or decrease (evidence of foam concentrate leakage) in the volume of the dyed water in the foam concentrate tank during flushing. If there is any volume change, the system shall be redesigned or repaired, as appropriate, and the test repeated until the system can be flushed without a gain or loss of liquid in the foam concentrate tank.

(7) The discharge range(s) shall show no signs of deterioration as additional applicators are engaged.

(8) The stabilized system discharge pressure shall not fluctuate by more than 10 percent when comparing the stabilized discharge pressure of the roof turret flowing by itself to the stabilized discharge pressure of the system with all appliances discharging simultaneously.

(9) Dye shall be evident in the stream discharging from all appliances at all times during the test.

(10) The ground sweep/bumper turret discharge rate shall be acceptable if it meets the criteria given in Paragraph 83 and Table 3, Performance Parameter 6.a or 7.a, as applicable.

(11) The ground sweep/bumper turret discharge range and pattern shall be acceptable if they meet the criteria given in Paragraph 83 and Table 3, Performance Parameter 6.b.(1) and (2) or 7.b.(1)-(3) and 7.c, as applicable.

(12) The handline discharge rate shall be acceptable if it meets the criteria of Paragraph 81 and the standards of Table 3, Performance Parameter 3.a or 4.a, as applicable.

(13) The handline discharge range and pattern shall be acceptable if they meet the criteria given in Paragraph 81 and the standards of Table 3, Performance Parameter 3.b and c or 4.b and c, as applicable.

NOTE: Handline discharge performance criteria are based on testing with the specified minimum length of hose; i.e., 100 feet of hard rubber/reeled hose or 150 feet (45m) of woven jacket hose. If additional lengths are requested, the minimum nozzle discharge rates must still be met. Hence, it is understood that higher discharge pressure at the hose inlet or larger diameter hose or both may be needed to meet the minimum nozzle discharge rate.

(14) The turret travel is acceptable if the horizontal and vertical travel angles and the turret stream near point of impact meet or exceed the criteria of Paragraph 84.a and b(1) through (3).

(15) The forces required to operate the turret shall be acceptable if they are equal to or less than those specified by Paragraph 84.c or d, as applicable.

(16) The turret discharge rate shall be acceptable if it meets or exceeds the criteria given in Paragraph 84.e and the standards of Table 3, Performance Parameter 5.a, as applicable to the vehicle class.

(17) The turret discharge range and pattern shall be acceptable if they meet or exceed the criteria given in Paragraph 84 and the standards of Table 3, Performance Parameter 5.b.(1) and (2), as applicable.

(18) The undertruck nozzle discharge performance shall be acceptable if it conforms to the requirements of Paragraph 85.

(19) There shall be no evidence of proportioning error, pressure surge/drops, or flow rate instability during the pump-and-roll tests.

(20) The operation of the pump shall not cause the engine to stall under any of the pump-and-roll test conditions.

(21) There shall be no evidence of unsafe vehicle dynamics (e.g., lurching, sudden speed changes, sudden forward/backward motion, or stops) resulting from the engagement/disengagement of the pumps during the pump and roll maneuvering or while the vehicle is stationary.

(22) There shall be no unsafe vehicle dynamics resulting from the engaging/disengaging of the vehicle drive.

(23) Foam solution or dye shall be evident in the discharge from all outlets operated during the pump and roll maneuvers.

(24) The foam concentrate proportioner system shall be acceptable if the foam solution concentration measured for each agent applicator, during individual and combined discharge, falls within the applicable standard tolerance range specified in Paragraph 76.

(25) The foam generation capability of the water/foam agent system shall be acceptable if the expansion ratio and 25-percent drainage time of the finished foam meet or exceed the criteria of Paragraph 87.b and d and the applicable standards of Table 3, when measured for each agent applicator during individual and combined discharge.

111. GRADABILITY.

a. Facilities.

(1) This test requires a site with a known grade of at least 50 percent that is long enough to allow the vehicle being tested to achieve a speed of 1 mph (1.6 km/h) with all wheels still on the grade.

(2) If the optional simulated grade/draw bar pull method is used, a level, paved site is required that can accommodate the combined length of the vehicle being tested and a load dynamometer sled while this combination achieves speeds up to 1 mph (1.6 km/h).

b. Equipment Required.

(1) If the alternate draw bar pull method is to be used, a load cell accurate to within ± 500 pounds (230 kg) and a variable load dynamometer sled will be needed.

(2) A test report notebook or similar record forms to be used as a test report worksheets and incorporated into the documentation package is required.

c. Test Conditions.

(1) The vehicle shall be fully loaded.

(2) The vehicle engine(s) and transmission shall be at normal operating temperature.

d. Test Procedures.

(1) **TEST 1. On Grade.** Position the vehicle on the flat at the bottom of the 50-percent grade, initiate ascent of the grade, and achieve a speed of at least 1 mph (1.6 km/h). Record the actual speed achieved.

(2) **TEST 1A. Alternate On Grade.**

NOTE: If an actual 50-percent grade is not available, the vehicle may be coupled to a "50-percent grade equivalent" draw bar load. The load cell reading (in unit force per unit area) required to simulate the 50-percent grade must equal:

$$\frac{\sin 26.57° \text{ x gross vehicle weight}}{\text{unit area of the load cell}}$$

(a) With the vehicle coupled to the appropriate simulated grade, initiate the simulated ascent of the grade, continue the forward motion, and monitor the load cell readings until a speed of at least 1 mph (1.6 km/h) is achieved.

(b) Record the load cell reading and the actual speed achieved.

e. Pass/Fail Criteria.
The vehicle performance shall be acceptable if the grade or simulated grade is negotiated smoothly and safely and the vehicle fulfills the standard requirements of Paragraph 55.

112. RADIO INTERFERENCE SUPPRESSION.

a. Facilities. Those specified in SAE J551/4 or an equivalent standard approved by the authority having jurisdiction.

b. Equipment Required.

(1) The equipment specified in SAE J551/4 or an equivalent standard approved by the authority having jurisdiction.

(2) A test report notebook or similar record forms to be used as a test report worksheet and incorporated into the documentation package.

c. Test Conditions.

(1) All electrical devices required by this specification shall be mounted on the vehicle and shall be operational.

(2) The vehicle engine(s) shall be operating at idle.

(3) All vehicle lighting shall be on.

(4) All heat, defrost, and air conditioning systems shall be operating with their respective fans operating at maximum speed.

(5) If provided, auxiliary power generating devices shall be running.

(6) All intermittent warning devices, such as overheat, low pressure or fluid level, high temperature, or vehicle backing warning buzzers—as well as hazard flashers, sirens, and horns—shall be turned off.

(7) All other vehicle-mounted electrical devices normally functioning at an accident site shall be turned on.

d. Test Procedure.

(1) Use the procedures required by SAE J551/4 or the equivalent standard.

(2) Record and evaluate the test results in accordance with SAE J551/4 or the equivalent test standard.

e. Pass/Fail Criteria. The radio interference suppression shall be acceptable if it meets the requirements of SAE J551/4 or the equivalent standard.

113. SIREN SOUND OUTPUT: DIRECTION AND MAGNITUDE.

a. Facilities. This test requires a flat open area where it is acceptable to generate a loud noise for an extended period of time. The area shall not have any large reflecting surfaces (e.g., other vehicles, storage tanks, hills, signboards, or buildings) within a 200-foot (60 m) radius of the test vehicle.

b. Equipment Required.

(1) A tape measure suitable for measuring 100 feet (30 m) with an accuracy of ± 1 inch and a protractor with an accuracy of ± 1 degree.

(2) A sound level meter calibrated within the past 12-month period by a certified testing laboratory. The meter shall meet the requirements of the American National Standards Institute (ANSI) Specifications for Type 2 Sound Level Meters SI.4-1971, or the latest revision.

(3) Sufficient sets of OSHA-approved ear protection devices for all test personnel.

(4) A test report notebook or similar record forms to be used as a test report work sheet and incorporated into the documentation package.

c. Test Conditions. The vehicle siren/siren speaker shall be mounted in its normal location and be fully operational.

d. Test Procedure.

(1) Measure and mark the locations for three listening posts, as follows:

(a) The first shall be at 45 degrees to the left of the longitudinal centerline of the vehicle and 100 feet (30 m) from the left corner of the front bumper.

(b) The second shall be on the centerline and 100 feet (30 m) in front of the front bumper.

(c) The third shall be 45 degrees to the right of the centerline and 100 feet (30 m) from the right corner of the front bumper.

(2) Set the sound level meter to the "A-weighing network, fast meter response."

(3) Place the sound level meter at one of the listening posts with the microphone located 5.5 feet (1.65 m) above the ground.

(4) Activate the siren and record the meter reading.

(5) Repeat steps (2) through (4) at the other two listening posts.

e. **Pass/Fail Criteria.** The siren shall be acceptable if the recorded sound levels meet or exceed the standards of Paragraph 8.a.(2).

114. STABILITY: DYNAMIC.

a. **Facilities.** The tests require a level, dry, paved surface at least 250 feet (75 m) in diameter and free from loose material. A 100-foot (30 m) radius circle that can be seen and followed by the vehicle driver shall be marked on the surface.

b. **Equipment Required.**

(1) A calibrated speedometer or other accurate speed measuring device.

(2) A means of measuring steering wheel cramp angle.

(3) An inclinometer capable of measuring the slope of the vehicle or the support surface during the tilting procedure with an accuracy of ± 0.5 degrees.

(4) A test report notebook or similar record forms to be used as a test report worksheet and incorporated into the documentation package.

c. **Test Conditions.**

(1) The vehicle shall be fully loaded.

(2) If the vehicle is equipped with a high-reach, extendible turret, it shall be retracted and secured in its stowed position during these tests.

d. **Test Procedure.**

(1) TEST 1. **Dynamic Turning Control.**

(a) Drive the vehicle at less than 1 mph (1.6 km/h) around the 100-foot (30 m) radius circle while keeping the centerline of the front of the vehicle approximately over the marked circle. After the driver has stabilized the vehicle on this path, place a reference mark on the steering wheel cramp angle indicator, and record the actual speed. To measure speed accurately, calculate the distance (circumference) that the vehicle travels and divide it by the time it takes to travel that distance.

(b) Gradually increase the vehicle speed until the maximum safe speed, as judged by the driver, is reached. Record the actual speed and steering wheel cramp angle.

(c) Repeat steps (a) and (b) while driving the vehicle in the opposite direction.

(3) TEST 2. **Cornering Stability.**

A speed, as outlined in the Table 2, shall be obtained and maintained for one full revolution of the circle in accordance with SAE J2181, as follows:

(a) Slowly drive the vehicle around the 150-foot (45-m) radius circle while keeping the centerline of the front of the vehicle directly over the marked line.

(b) Establish a reference position on the steering wheel position indicator at a slow speed.

(c) Gradually increase the speed until the maximum safe speed, as judged by the driver, is reached.

(d) Record the maximum speed and the corresponding position of the steering wheel.

(e) Repeat steps (a) through (d) while driving the vehicle in the opposite direction.

The speed achieved shall be greater than 22 mph (35 km/h) for all classes of vehicles, and the steering angle shall not decrease with increasing speed. The truck shall have neither oversteer nor understeer characteristics in this test.

(4) TEST 3. **Evasive Maneuver Test (North Atlantic Treaty Organization (NATO) Lane Change).** A double lane change test shall be conducted in accordance with NATO AVTP 03-160W, Dynamic Stability. The vehicle shall be driven through the cones at 35 mph (56 km/h) without loss of control or vehicle stability in two directions. The vehicle shall not display oversteer or understeer conditions.

e. **Pass/Fail Criteria.** The dynamic turning control of the vehicle shall be acceptable if it meets the criteria of Paragraph 53 and the standard in Table 2, Performance Parameter 3, and the steering angle required to keep the vehicle on the circular path shall not decrease at any time with increasing speed; i.e., oversteer characteristics are unacceptable.

115. STEERING SYSTEM: RESISTANCE AND TURNING DIAMETER.

   a. Facilities. These tests require a dry, level, paved area that is free from loose material and is larger in all directions than three times the length of the vehicle being tested.

   b. Equipment Required.

   (1) A spring scale or another means of measuring the force applied to the steering wheel rim with an accuracy of ± 2 percent of the value being measured.

   (2) A set of wheel chocks.

   (3) A device suitable for measuring three times the length of the vehicle being tested with an accuracy of ± 1 inch (25.4mm).

   (4) Marking devices suitable for marking the pavement.

   (5) A plumb bob or other device suitable for locating a point on the pavement directly below a fixed point on the vehicle.

   (6) A test report notebook or similar record forms to be used as a test report worksheet and incorporated into the documentation package.

   c. Test Conditions.

   (1) The vehicle shall be fully loaded.

   (2) The vehicle steering system shall be fully operational, and the steering linkage stops shall be adjusted to the manufacturer's specified production tolerance limits.

   d. Test Procedure.

   (1) TEST 1. Resistance or Operating Force Requirements.

   (a) With wheel chocks under one set of nonsteering wheels, set the steerable wheels in the straight ahead position, start the engine, engage neutral, and release the brakes. Ensure that the vehicle does not roll.

   (b) With the engine at idle speed, measure and record the forces needed at the steering wheel rim to move the steering linkage from center to full left and full right stops. Also measure the force

required to move the steering wheel from full left stop to full right stop and visa versa.

   (2) TEST 2. Wall-to-Wall Turning Diameter.

   (a) Drive the vehicle slowly in a full cramp circle (left or right) to establish a steady state in the steering linkage.

   (b) Continue driving the slow full cramp circle.

   (c) At approximately three equidistant points (identified as A, B, and C) around the circle, gently stop the vehicle using the service brakes.

   (d) At each stop, place a plumb bob against the outermost point of the vehicle, and mark the spot on the ground directly below where the plumb bob comes to rest.

   (e) Measure and record the straight line distances between each pair of points; e.g., Lengths AB, BC, and CA.

   (f) Calculate the wall-to-wall turning diameter (D), as follows:

Where: D = 2R and

$$\text{Length S} = \frac{[AB + BC + CA]}{2}$$

$$D = 2R = \frac{AB \times BC \times CA}{2 \times [S \times (S\text{-}AB) \times (S\text{-}BC) \times (S\text{-}CA)]^{1/2}}$$

   (g) Repeat steps (a) through (f) with the vehicle moving in the opposite direction.

   e. Pass/Fail Criteria.

   (1) The steering system operating forces shall be acceptable if they meet the standards specified in Paragraph 33.a and b.

   (2) The steering turning radius shall be acceptable if it meets the wall-to-wall turning diameter (D or 2R) standard specified in Paragraph 33.d and Table 2, Performance Parameter 8.

116. UNDERBODY CLEARANCES.

   a. Facilities. This test requires a dry, level, paved area that is free from loose material and large enough to accommodate the vehicle being tested.

b. Required Equipment.

(1) A device suitable for measuring the vehicle length with an accuracy of ± 0.25 inches (63 mm).

(2) A large protractor suitable for measuring angles with an accuracy of ± 0.5 degree.

(3) A test report notebook or similar record forms to be used as a test report worksheet and incorporated into the documentation package.

c. Test Conditions. The vehicle shall be fully loaded.

d. Test Procedure.

(1) Position the vehicle on the test area, and measure the following dimensions in accordance with their definitions as stated in Appendix 1:

    (a) Angle of Approach.

    (b) Angle of Departure.

    (c) Interaxle Clearance Angle.

    (d) Underbody Clearance.

    (e) Underaxle Clearance.

(2) The results of the linear dimensions shall be rounded down to the nearest 0.5 inches (1.25 cm) and recorded.

(3) The results of the angular dimensions shall be rounded down to the nearest 0.5 degrees and recorded.

e. Pass/Fail Criteria. The underbody clearances shall be acceptable if they meet the standards of Table 2, Performance Parameters 4 through 7, for the applicable vehicle class.

117. VISIBILITY: INCLUDED ANGLES FROM THE DRIVER'S SEAT.

a. Facilities. This test requires a level site located in a dimly lit or heavily shaded area that is at least 20 feet (6.1 m) longer than the vehicle to be tested. Testing may also be performed in the low light of early morning or late evening hours.

b. Equipment Required.

(1) A device suitable for measuring distances up to 50 feet (15 m) with an accuracy of ±0.25 inch (63 mm).

(2) A large protractor suitable for measuring angles with an accuracy of ± 0.5 degree.

(3) A plumb bob or other device suitable for establishing a vertical reference point.

(4) A small, sharply focused light source (e.g., flashlight, electric pointer, or other light source suitable for establishing the "line of sight" under the available test light conditions.

(5) A device capable of holding the light source that can be adjusted vertically and horizontally to serve as the simulated driver eye location on the driver's seat.

(6) A test report notebook or similar record forms to be used as a test report worksheet and incorporated into the documentation package.

c. Test Conditions. The vehicle shall be fully loaded.

d. Test Procedure.

(1) Adjust the driver's seat to its mid position, with respect to top surface height and the fore and aft adjustment, and place approximately 175 pounds (80 kg) on the seat. Adjust the rake of the seat back to the vertical.

(2) Place the eye location device in the driver's seat, and adjust it so as to locate the simulated focal point 31.75 inches (80 cm) above the seat surface and 6 inches (15 cm) in front of the vertical plane of the front surface of the seat back.

(3) Identify the upper and lower limits of the line of sight in the forward direction by moving the light beam in the vertical direction until it just touches those obstructions.

(4) Measure and record the angle above and below the straight ahead focal plane where vision first becomes obstructed.

(5) Measure and record the distance along the ground from a point directly below the front surface of the front bumper to the point on the ground that is intersected by the light beam at the lowest angle of visibility.

(6) Identify restrictions to the extreme left and right lines of sight by moving the light beam in the horizontal direction until it just touches those obstructions.

(7) Measure and record the angles left and right of the straight ahead line of sight where vision first becomes obstructed.

(8) At the extreme left and right visibility limits, measure and record the angle below the horizontal focal plane where downward vision first becomes obstructed.

(9) At the extreme left and right visibility limits, measure and record the distance along the ground from a point directly below the vehicle surface (that is on the line of sight) to the point on the ground that is intersected by the light beam at the lowest angle of visibility.

(10) Repeat step 9 as necessary to establish a reasonably smooth arc of visibility between the extreme left point and the center point (established in step 6) and between the center point and the extreme right point.

e. Pass/Fail Criteria. Driver visibility from the cab shall be acceptable if it meets the standards of Paragraph 28.d.(1) through (5).

118. VEHICLE INTERIOR NOISE LEVEL.

a. Facilities. This test requires that the vehicle be parked at a location where no large reflecting surfaces—such as other vehicles, signboards, buildings, or hills—are within 50 feet (15 m) of the driver's seating position.

b. Equipment Required. A sound level meter meeting the requirements of the ANSI S1.4-1971, Specification for Sound Level Meters, for Type 2 Meters.

c. Test Conditions.

(1) Test the vehicle in fully loaded conditions and at normal operating temperatures. Ensure engine radiator fans and/or other thermostatically controlled shutters are functioning normally. If the vehicle cannot achieve performance parameters with the fan(s) operating, review power requirements.

(2) Park the vehicle in a location that meets the criteria of Paragraph a. above.

(3) The driver shall be in the normal seated position at the vehicle's controls.

(4) No other occupants, except the person conducting the test, shall be in the cab during the test.

d. Test Procedure.

(1) Set the sound meter to the A-weighting network, "fast" meter response.

(2) Locate the microphone, oriented vertically upward, 6 inches (15cm) to the right of, in the same plane as, and directly in line with the driver's right ear.

(3) If the engine is equipped with a governor, put the transmission in neutral and accelerate the engine to the maximum governed speed; OR if it is not equipped with an engine governor, accelerate to the speed for maximum rated horsepower. Stabilize the engine at that speed.

(4) Observe the "A-weighted" sound level reading on the meter for the stabilized engine speed condition. If the reading is not being influenced by extraneous noise sources, such as motor vehicles operating on adjacent roadways, record that reading.

(5) Reduce engine speed to idle and repeat the procedures specified in Paragraph d.(3) and (4) above until two maximum sound levels within 2 dB(A) of each other are recorded. Numerically average the two maximum sound level readings, and report the result as the vehicle's interior sound level at the driver's seating position.

e. Pass/Fail Criteria. The interior vehicle noise level shall be acceptable if the average noise level measured in accordance with the procedures above meets the criteria of Paragraph 28.e. A 2 dB(A) tolerance over that noise level limitation is permitted to allow for variations in test conditions and variations in the capabilities of meters.

119. STABILITY: STATIC/SIDE SLOPE (TILT TABLE).
The manufacturer shall conduct a static/side slope (tilt table) test on each prototype vehicle in accordance with the test procedure described in Paragraph 133.

120. RESERVED.

Section 4. Production Vehicle Performance Acceptance Tests.

121.   PRODUCTION TEST LIST. The ARFF vehicle manufacturer shall conduct the tests listed below on every vehicle. These tests may be conducted at the manufacturer's facility, at the airport, or at another mutually acceptable test site. Paragraphs 122 through 134 detail specific facilities, equipment, test conditions, test procedures, and the pass/fail criteria for each function to be tested. The purchaser shall be afforded the opportunity to witness production tests.

    a.   Acceleration.

    b.   Air compressor capacity.

    c.   Balance/weight distribution.

    d.   Brake control.

    e.   Water/foam proportioner(s) tolerance.

    f.   Water/foam solution pump discharge stability.

    g.   Dual pump discharge stability.

    h.   Pressure test of piping and connections.

    i.   Pump and roll capability.

    j.   Roof turret discharge rate.

    k.   Top speed.

    l.   Stability: Static/Side Slope (Tilt Table)

    m.   Piercing/Penetration Nozzle Testing.

122.   ACCELERATION.

    a.   Facilities. This test requires a dry, straight, level paved surface of sufficient length to accelerate the vehicle from 0 to 50 mph (0 to 80 km/h) and to bring it to a safe stop. Sufficient space is needed at each end to turn and reposition the vehicle for a return run.

    b.   Equipment Required.

        (1) The vehicle speedometer and tachometer as installed.

        (2) A stopwatch that can be read to ± 0.5 second.

        (3) A test report notebook or similar record forms to be used as a test report worksheet and incorporated into the documentation package.

    c.   Test Conditions.

        (1) Conduct the test at any elevation between sea level and 2,000 feet (600 m) unless otherwise specified by the purchaser.

        (2) The vehicle shall be fully loaded.

        (3) The engine(s) and transmission(s) shall be at normal operating temperature.

    d.   Test Procedure.

        (1) Start with the vehicle at rest, the engine at idle, and the transmission in gear. No "windup" of the drive trains shall be permitted.

        (2) Simultaneously start the stopwatch and begin accelerating the vehicle. Continue accelerating at full throttle until the vehicle reaches 50 mph (80 km/h), stop the watch, and decelerate/brake to a safe stop.

        (3) Record the elapsed time.

        (4) Repeat this test sequence in the opposite direction to cancel the effects of wind and slope. Take at least three readings in each direction. Calculate and report the average acceleration rate.

    e.   Pass/fail criteria. The acceleration shall be acceptable if the reported average acceleration time meets or is less than the standard of Table 2, Performance Parameter 9.

123.   AIR COMPRESSOR CAPACITY.

    a.   Facilities. None.

    b.   Equipment Required.

        (1) The vehicle air system pressure gauge(s) as installed.

        (2) A stopwatch that can be read to ± 0.5 second.

        (3) A test report notebook or similar record forms to be used as a test report worksheet and incorporated into the documentation package.

c. **Test Conditions.**

(1) The vehicle air system shall be fully operational.

(2) The engine shall be turned off at the start.

(3) The transmission shall be in neutral.

(4) The parking brake shall be set.

(5) The ratio of the actual volume of the installed air reservoir to the minimum required reservoir volume specified in Paragraph 32.a.(2) shall have been or must now be established.

(6) The minimum spring brake release pressure must be known.

d. **Test Procedure.**

(1) Bleed off air reservoir pressure by operating the service brake until the vehicle air gauge(s) indicate less than 85 psi (5.9 Bar).

(2) Start the engine and increase speed to maximum governed rpm. Monitor the increase in air pressure. When the pressure reaches 85 psi (5.9 Bar), start the stopwatch. If there is more than one air pressure gauge, start the time when the first gauge indicates 85 psi (5.9 Bar).

(3) Continue monitoring the pressure increase until a minimum of 100 psi (6.9 Bar) is indicated on all gauges; stop the stopwatch, shut off the engine, and record the time.

(4) Bleed off air reservoir pressure by operating the service brake until all vehicle air gauge(s) indicate less than 5 psi (0.3 Bar).

(5) Start engine and increase speed to maximum governed rpm. Monitor the increase in air pressure. When the gauge for the quick buildup system reaches 5 psi (0.3 Bar), start the stopwatch.

(6) Continue monitoring the pressure increase until the gauge for the quick buildup system reaches the value established for the spring brake release pressure; stop the stopwatch, shut off the engine, and verify that the spring brake release will function at that pressure. Record the time.

e. **Pass/Fail Criteria.**

(1) The acceptable time for pressure in the brake air system reservoir to build from 85 psi to 100 psi (5.9 to 6.9 Bar) shall be 25 seconds or less; or

(2) If the volume of the reservoir provided is greater than the minimum required by Paragraph 32.a.(2)(a), a proportionately longer buildup time shall be acceptable. Calculate the allowed time using the formula provided in the referenced paragraph.

(3) The acceptable time for the quick buildup system to reach the pressure necessary for spring brake release shall be 12 seconds or less.

124. BALANCE/WEIGHT DISTRIBUTION.

a. **Facilities.**

(1) This test requires an inground vehicle scale that is large enough to accommodate the vehicle and has a certified accuracy of ± 1 percent of the weighed amount.

(2) A clean, level area suitable for positioning the vehicle on a set of portable wheel scales.

b. **Equipment Required.**

(1) The inground scales described above.

(2) A set of certified wheel scales with an accuracy of ±1 percent.

(3) A test report notebook or similar record forms to be used as a test report worksheet and incorporated into the documentation package.

c. **Test Conditions.**

(1) The vehicle shall be fully loaded.

(2) The vehicle shall be free of any accumulations of snow, ice, mud, or other material that could be "seen" within the accuracy limits of the scales.

d. **Test Procedure.**

(1) Measure the gross vehicle weight (GVW).

(2) Measure the load on each axle at the ground.

NOTE: Measuring the GVW all at once on an inground scale will be more accurate than taking the sum of the individual axle measurements. Hence, the individual axle loads shall be proportionately corrected as needed to make the sum of their loads agree with the GVW measurement.

(3) Measure the load at the ground on each tire.

NOTE: Proportionate corrections shall be made to these results as needed to make the sum of their loads agree with the corrected load on the respective axle.

(4) Make the following calculations, using the results of the measurements made above.

(a) The percent difference in axle load between the lightest and the heaviest axle load:

$$\frac{\text{Heaviest Axle Ld - Lightest Axle Ld x 100}}{\text{Heaviest Axle Load}} = \underline{\hspace{1cm}}\%$$

(b) The average tire load for each axle:

$$\frac{\text{Wt. on Right Tire(s) + Wt On Left Tire(s)}}{2} = \underline{\hspace{1cm}}\text{Load}$$

(c) The percent difference in tire load between the average tire load for a given axle and the difference between the heaviest and the lightest tire load for that axle (calculate for each axle):

$$\frac{\text{Heaviest Tire Ld - Lightest Tire Ld x 100}}{\text{Average Tire Ld for Axle}} = \underline{\hspace{1cm}}\%$$

e.   Pass/Fail Criteria.

(1) The GVW shall be acceptable if it does not exceed the vehicle manufacturer's gross vehicle rating. The axle manufacturer's published axle ratings shall not be increased to meet this requirement.

(2) The difference between the heaviest axle load and the lightest axle load shall be acceptable if it is no more than 10 percent of the heaviest axle load.

(3) The front axle shall not be the most heavily loaded axle.

EXCEPTION: The front axle may be the most heavily loaded in those cases where options specified by the purchaser cannot be practically engineered to conform with this requirement. However, if the front axle is the most heavily loaded, the difference between the front axle load and any other axle load shall not exceed 5 percent. In addition, none of the component ratings shall be exceeded to accommodate this deviation in the

balance/weight distribution, and all other performance requirements of this specification shall be met.

(4) The load difference between the tires on a given axle shall be no more than 5 percent of the average tire load for that axle.

125.   BRAKING CONTROL.

a.   Facilities.   This test requires the same facilities as Prototype Brake System Performance Test given in Paragraph 106.a.(2) or (3).

b.   Equipment Required.

(1) The speedometer, as installed by the vehicle manufacturer.

(2) A tape measure that can be read to ± 0.5 inches (1.25 cm).

(3) A test report notebook or similar record forms to be used as a test report worksheet and incorporated into the documentation package.

c.   Test Conditions.   The conditions are the same as those used for Prototype Brake System Performance, given in Paragraph 106.c.(2) through (6).

d.   Test Procedure.

(1) Start the vehicle, accelerate to 20 mph (32 km/h) and maintain a constant speed for at least 50 feet (15 m).

(2) Apply the service brake as if in a panic stop; hold the brake on until the vehicle stops.

NOTE: During the panic stop test, the driver shall make no steering corrections for vehicle drift during the stop.

(3) In a test lane with outer edge markings, measure and record the perpendicular distance from the nearest edge line to the outermost edge of the width of the vehicle. Report the measurement as a negative number if the vehicle is outside of the test lane.

(4) In a test lane with a marked centerline, measure and record the perpendicular distance from the centerline to the outermost edge of the width of the vehicle that is farthest from the centerline of the test lane.

(5) Repeat steps 1 through 4 above, EXCEPT at a constant speed of 40 mph (64 km/h).

e. **Pass/Fail Criteria.**

(1) Braking control in a lane with outer boundary markers shall be acceptable if NO portion of the vehicle is outside those boundaries when the vehicle stops.

(2) Braking control in a lane with a marked centerline shall be acceptable if the measured distance is equal to or less than one-half of the vehicle width plus 2 feet (60 cm) when the vehicle stops.

126. WATER/FOAM PROPORTIONER(S) TOLERANCE.

NOTE: This test may be combined with the test in Paragraph 127.

a. **Facilities.** This test requires an open area suitable for discharging a modest volume of water/foam solution at high pressure.

b. **Equipment Required.** The same equipment as required for the Foam Proportioning/Foam Concentrate Test ("refractometer test") performed in accordance with NFPA 412.

c. **Test Conditions.**

(1) All water/foam applicator discharge system performance requirements shall have been previously verified by prototype tests, as specified in Paragraph 105.

(2) Provide the same conditions as for Water/foam Agent System Prototype Test given in Paragraphs 110.c.(1), (3), (4), (5), and (6).

NOTE: Test and evaluate foam proportioner tolerance at the fixed, minimum acceptable rate per Table 3 for each type of applicator.

d. **Test Procedure.** The test procedure is the same as for Water/foam Agent System Prototype Test given in Paragraph 110.d, Test 17, except that only the test for foam concentration ("refractometer test") shall be performed.

e. **Pass/Fail Criteria.** The foam concentrate proportioner system shall be acceptable if the foam solution concentration measured for each agent applicator, during individual and combined discharge and at the minimum acceptable discharge rate specified in Table 3 for each type of applicator, is within the standard range specified in Paragraph 76.

127. WATER/FOAM SOLUTION PUMP DISCHARGE STABILITY.

NOTE: This test may be combined with the test in Paragraph 126.

a. **Facilities.**

(1) This test requires an open site suitable for discharging large volumes of water/foam solution at high pressure.

(2) The site must provide access to water and a supply of foam concentrate sufficient to refill vehicle tanks.

b. **Equipment Required.**

(1) Vehicle pump engine tachometer and agent system discharge pressure gauge, as installed by the manufacturer.

(2) A test report notebook or similar record forms to be used as a test report worksheet and incorporated into the documentation package.

c. **Test Conditions.**

(1) All water/foam applicator discharge system performance requirements shall have been previously verified by prototype tests, as specified in Paragraph 105.

(2) The agent system pressure relief valve shall have been previously verified as being set to the recommended relief pressure.

(3) The temperature of the water and the foam concentrate shall be within the foam manufacturer's recommended operating temperature range.

(4) Ensure the water and the foam tanks are full at the start.

(5) Set the foam concentrate proportioners at the appropriate rate for the foam concentrate to be used at the airport.

(6) Set the agent selector for water/foam discharge.

(7) All primary handlines shall be fully deployed.

(8) Set all applicator nozzles for straight stream.

(9) If the vehicle is equipped with multiple pumps, they should be operated in parallel during this test.

d. Test Procedure.

(1) Start the vehicle pump engine and bring it up to maximum recommended operating rpm.

(2) Engage the agent pump(s) and bring it up to maximum pumping pressure with all agent applicator outlets closed. Observe and record pump discharge pressure.

(3) Adjust roof turret elevation to optimum range position and open the roof turret discharge valve. Observe the range of turret stream, continue flow to allow system pressure to stabilize, and observe and record pressure.

(4) Continue turret discharge, and initiate discharge from each of the following in turn: ground sweep or bumper turret, primary handlines (add one at a time), and undertruck nozzles (if provided). All applicators shall be discharging simultaneously in a straight stream.

NOTE: As each additional applicator is turned on, the range of the initial turret stream and the initial range of each added appliance stream should be compared by observation and the system pressure observed and, after system pressure stabilization, record the pressure.

(5) Continue discharging with all applicators flowing until the system pressure has stabilized; then record pressure and stop test.

e. Pass/Fail Criteria.

(1) The discharge range(s) shall show no signs of deterioration as additional applicators are engaged.

(2) The stabilized system discharge pressure shall not fluctuate by more than 10 percent when comparing the stabilized discharge pressure of the roof turret flowing by itself to the stabilized discharge pressure of the system with all appliances discharging simultaneously.

(3) Foam shall be evident in the discharge stream of all appliances at all times during the test.

128. DUAL PUMP DISCHARGE STABILITY.

NOTE: This test shall be performed only on those vehicles that are equipped with dual pumps and only

after they have satisfactorily completed the "Water/foam Solution Pump Discharge Stability" test requirements of Paragraph 127.

a. Facilities. Same as Paragraph 127.a.

b. Equipment Required. The same equipment specified in Paragraph 127.b.

c. Test Conditions.

(1) All water/foam applicator discharge system performance requirements shall have been previously verified by prototype tests, as specified in Paragraph 105.

(2) The agent system pressure relief valve shall have been previously verified as being set to the recommended relief pressure and operable.

(3) If the vehicle is equipped with multiple pumps, they shall be operated in parallel during the first half of this test.

d. Test Procedure.

(1) Use the same procedures outlined in Paragraph 127.d.(1) through (5).

(2) Disengage pump number one, and repeat the test.

(3) Repeat the test using only pump number one.

e. Pass/Fail Criteria.

(1) The discharge range(s) shall show no signs of deterioration as additional applicators are engaged.

(2) The stabilized system discharge pressure shall not fluctuate by more than 10 percent when comparing the stabilized discharge pressure of the roof turret flowing by itself to the stabilized discharge pressure of the system with all appliances discharging simultaneously.

(3) Foam shall be evident in the discharge stream of all appliances at all times during the test.

(4) There shall be no more than 50 ± 2 percent pressure difference in the stabilized agent system when operating on one pump as compared to two.

129. PRESSURE TEST OF PIPING AND CONNECTIONS.

  a. Facilities.

  (1) This test requires access to dry compressed air or nitrogen.

  (2) The test area shall also provide sufficient clearance between the vehicle being tested and any other valuable property so as to preclude damage in the event of a pipe or fitting failure.

  (3) The test area shall also provide for appropriate protection for the test personnel against possible flying debris from a component failure.

  b. Equipment Required.

  (1) A gauge suitable for the intended service with an accuracy of ± 5 psi and a working range equal to 2.0 times the normal agent system operating pressure.

  (2) A means of developing and delivering pressure equal to 1.5 times the normal agent system operating pressure.

  (3) Miscellaneous plates, caps, and fittings suitable for isolating the suction side of the agent system, if necessary, and a suitable leak detection solution.

  (4) A test report notebook or similar record forms to be used as a test report worksheet and incorporated into the documentation package.

  c. Test Conditions.

NOTE: It is often easier and/or more convenient to perform this test before the vehicle body is completely assembled with the agent system controls in place. Therefore, the agent system does not have to be fully operational for this test.

  (1) The agent system piping shall be fully assembled; i.e., no subsystem testing is permitted.

  (2) Isolate all suction side piping components that cannot tolerate the test pressures from the discharge system.

  (3) Include agent pumps in the discharge system test.

  (4) Close all agent discharge outlet valves.

  (5) Block all bypass lines from the discharge system to the water and foam concentrate tanks during the test.

  (6) Fill the agent pumps and all discharge piping with water.

  d. Test Procedure.

  (1) Pressurize the agent discharge system to at least 1.5 times the maximum recommended system operating pressure.

  (2) Isolate the agent discharge system in the pressurized condition by closing the test pressure supply line inlet valve and lowering the supply device pressure.

  (3) Record the pressure and monitor the system pressure for at least 30 minutes.

  (4) If the pressure drops, locate and repair the leaks, and repeat the test until the pressure can be maintained for at least 30 minutes.

  (5) Upon completion of the test, remove any discharge/suction system isolation devices and reassemble the suction piping.

  (6) Fill the water and foam concentrate tanks, and inspect the suction piping for leaks during and immediately after the agent system has been operated in the water/foam solution discharge mode.

  e. Pass/Fail Criteria.

  (1) No pressure decay shall be permitted during the 30-minute pressure holding period.

  (2) No leaks shall be permitted in the discharge or suction piping during or after agent system operation.

130. PUMP AND ROLL CAPABILITY.

  a. Facilities. Use the same facilities as used for the Water/foam Agent System Prototype Test given in Paragraph 110.a.(1), (2), and (4).

  b. Equipment Required. The same equipment as required for the Water/foam Agent System Prototype Test given in Paragraph 110.b.(2), (6), and (11).

  c. Test Conditions.

  (1) The vehicle agent system shall be fully operational.

(2) All water/foam applicator discharge system performance requirements shall have been previously verified by prototype tests, as specified in Paragraph 105.

(3) Use the same conditions as provided for the Water/foam Agent System Prototype Test, described in Paragraph 110.c.(1) and (3) through (8).

d.   Test Procedure. Use the same procedure as for the Water/foam Agent System Prototype Tests 14 and 15, outlined in Paragraph 110.d.

e.   Pass/Fail Criteria. The pass/fail criteria is the same as used for the Water/foam Agent System Prototype Tests 14 and 15, given in Paragraph 110.e.(19) through (23).

131.   ROOF TURRET DISCHARGE RATE.

a.   Facilities. Use the same facilities as for the Water/foam Agent System Prototype Tests 11 or 11A, Paragraph 110.a.(1) and (4).

b.   Equipment Required. The same equipment as for the Water/foam Agent System Prototype Tests 11 or 11A, Paragraph 110.b.(2), (3), (4), (7), (8), and (11).

c.   Test Conditions.

(1) The vehicle agent system shall be fully operational.

(2) All water/foam applicator discharge system performance requirements shall have been previously verified by prototype tests as specified in Paragraph 105.

(3) Provide the same conditions described in Paragraph 110.c.(1) and (3) through (8).

d.   Test Procedure. Follow the same procedures outlined in Paragraph 110.d.

e.   Pass/Fail Criteria. Same as for the Water/foam Agent System Prototype Tests 11 or 11A, given in Paragraph 110.e.(16).

132.   TOP SPEED.

a.   Facilities. This test requires a dry, straight, level, paved surface of sufficient length to accelerate the vehicle to 65 mph (104 km/h) and to bring it safely to a rapid stop. Sufficient space is needed at each end to turn and reposition the vehicle for a return run.

b.   Equipment Required.

(1) The vehicle speedometer and tachometer, as installed.

(2) A test report notebook or similar record forms to be used as a test report worksheet and incorporated into the documentation package.

c.   Test Conditions.

(1) Conduct the test at an elevation between sea level and up to 2,000 feet (600 m) unless otherwise specified by the purchaser.

(2) Ensure the vehicle is fully loaded.

(3) The engine(s) and the transmission(s) shall be at normal operating temperature.

d.   Test Procedure.

(1) Start with the vehicle at rest, the engine at idle, and the transmission in gear.

(2) Simultaneously start the stopwatch and begin accelerating the vehicle. Continue accelerating at full throttle until the vehicle reaches at least 65 mph (104 km/h). Record the speed actually achieved.

(3) Repeat this test sequence in the opposite direction to cancel the effects of wind and slope. At least two readings in each direction shall be taken to calculate the reported average top speed.

e.   Pass/Fail Criteria. The reported average top speed shall be acceptable if it meets or exceeds the standards specified in Paragraph 57.

133.   STABILITY: STATIC/SIDE SLOPE (TILT TABLE).

a.   Facilities.

(1) Test 2 requires a tilt table or other suitable surface capable of being tilted and on which the entire vehicle can be placed.

(2) Test 2 requires a means to restrain the vehicle at the balance point.

b.   Equipment Required. The same equipment as specified in Paragraph 114.b.

c.   Test Conditions. The same test conditions in Paragraph 114.c shall be applied.

d.   Test Procedure.

(1) Tilt the tethered vehicle to an angle at least equal to the side slope angle specified in Table 2, Performance Parameter 2, for the appropriate vehicle class.

(2) Once the vehicle is at the required angle, check the tether lines for tension. If there is tension, reduce the angle until the tension is relieved, and record the actual angle achieved.

NOTE: This test shall be accomplished with all requested equipment properly placed and installed as ordered by the end user. The tilt table angle shall be recorded on a metal data plate affixed to the left-hand door of the vehicle. This data plate shall list the following items: vehicle empty weight, maximum gross weight, special equipment installed prior to test, and front and rear axle weights with weight distribution calculation. The actual tilt table angle achieved in the test shall be recorded on the plate for left and right directions.

at maximum flow rate for the class of vehicle being tested.

e.   Pass/Fail Criteria. The static side slope stability of the vehicle shall be acceptable if it can stand on the applicable standard grade specified in Table 2, Performance Parameter 2, with no perceptible tension on the tether lines.

134. PIERCING/PENETRATION   NOZZLE TESTING.

a. Operational demonstration: The manufacturer shall demonstrate the ability to penetrate a sandwiched metal sample of two pieces of .090 5052-grade soft aluminum material with the penetration device in under 3 seconds.

b. The manufacturer shall demonstrate the ability to penetrate a sandwiched metal sample of two pieces of .090 2024-T3-grade aircraft aluminum in under 3 seconds.

(3) This test shall be conducted on a tilt table facility meeting SAE J2180 (Dec. 1998), A Tilt Table Procedure for Measuring the Static Rollover Threshold for Heavy Trucks. This tilt table shall contain a suitable surface, such as "open grid deck" material, to resist vehicle traction slippage without impacting the tilt table angle achieved. Restrain and tilt the vehicle until the vehicle tilt or side slope angle can be positively determined.

(4) Test the vehicle in its fully loaded condition with tires inflated to their recommended operating pressure. Use suitable ballast in place of the crew for safety.

(5) Where the vehicle is fitted with an extendable turret, perform an additional test, as follows:

Tilt the vehicle on a table, or position the vehicle on a 20-percent grade. Elevate the extendable turret to the highest elevation. Position the turret nozzle uphill at maximum horizontal rotation, and discharge the agent

c. A penetrator pointed nozzle shall be provided with a minimum flow rate of 250 gallons per minutes. The nozzle system shall be constructed to direct or spray agent and water on both sides of the aircraft at the same time after the penetration is made. (Concept-delivery shall be multiple holes causing a spray to cover 25 to 30 feet each side of the aircraft interior and aircraft aisleway.) The penetration shall take place in under 3 seconds of point contact and provide water to the floor and ceiling levels beyond the overhead storage bin area. (The proposed concept would be to penetrate above overwing window areas, above interior seat back height and below baggage storage bins. The penetration shall provide water extinguishment from ceiling to floor for a distance of 30 to 40 feet along the fuselage left and right of the centerline of the penetration point, thus stopping fire growth and protecting the interior until other vehicles can extinguish the outside exterior fuel fire.)

This Page Intentionally Left Blank

Appendix 1. DEFINITIONS.

Section 1. Introduction.

1. Aircraft rescue and fire fighting (ARFF) is a relatively new branch of the fire fighting profession. There are approximately 1 million paid, part-time, and volunteer firefighters in the United States and Canada. Thousands of new members who are unfamiliar with basic fire service terminology join the ranks each year. The unique terms used by airport firefighters in the performance of their duties further complicate the communications problem. Because of the small number of firefighters at most civil airports, airport/community disaster plans and the various mutual aid arrangements must involve many traditional structural firefighters. In order to work effectively together, these mixed forces must understand each other.

2. It is recognized that many geographical and technical dialects exist among fire service personnel and consultants. Hence, the terms in this appendix were assembled from a variety of individuals and institutions.

A special effort was made to observe precedence in usage. That is, where a recognized authority such as the International Civil Aviation Organization, the National Fire Protection Association, the National Transportation Safety Board, the Federal Aviation Administration, the structural fire service, or a specific equipment industry has historically used a word or phrase with a widely accepted meaning, it was adopted for use in this guide specification and is included in this appendix to encourage universal use and to enhance understanding.

3. No attempt has been made to include words that are clearly understood by qualified firefighters and non-firefighters alike or the many unique words that seem to be related only to structural fire fighting activities. Instead, the list is limited to the words and phrases that are most associated with aircraft rescue and fire fighting activities and aircraft rescue and fire fighting vehicles.

Section 2. Definitions

4. Acceptance Tests. Tests conducted on every vehicle by the manufacturer to assure that—

    a. Each vehicle is fully operational when delivered.

    b. The original level of performance verified by the prototype vehicle tests continues.

5. AFFF. (Spoken "A triple F") See Aqueous Film-Forming Foam Concentrate.

6. Aggressive Tire Tread. Tread designed to provide a maximum of traction for most types of service.

7. Air-Cooled Engine. One in which removal of waste heat from the cylinder walls is by direct transfer to the atmosphere by a moving air stream.

8. Air-Mechanical Brakes. Brakes in which the force from an individual air chamber directly applies the force to the friction surfaces through a mechanical linkage.

9. Air Over Hydraulic Brakes. Brakes in which the force of a master air cylinder applies the force to the friction surfaces through an intervening hydraulic system.

10. Ambient Temperature. The temperature of the environment surrounding a vehicle at any given time.

11. Angle of Approach or Departure. Describes the steepest ramp that a fully loaded vehicle can approach and ascend (or descend and depart) from a connecting horizontal surface without interference from any part of the vehicle. It is the angle bounded by the horizontal ground line and the line tangent to the loaded radius of the front/rear tire and the first structural part or vehicle accessory that it encounters as the angle increases above the horizontal.

12. Approved. Acceptable to the "authority having jurisdiction."

13. Aqueous Film-Forming Foam (AFFF) Concentrate. A concentrated aqueous solution of fluorinated surfactants and foam stabilizers that, when mixed with water in designated proportions, is capable of producing an aqueous fluorocarbon film on the surface of hydrocarbon fuels.

14. Authority Having Jurisdiction. The organization, office, or individual responsible for "approving" equipment, an installation, or a procedure.

15. Automatic Locking Differential. A type of non-slip differential that operates automatically.

16. Axle Tread. The distance between the center of two tires or wheels on the opposite ends of one axle.

17. Bogie. A tandem arrangement of aircraft or ground vehicle wheels and axles. The bogie axles can move semi-independently so all wheels follow the ground as the attitude of the aircraft or vehicle changes or the ground surface changes. For example, in a 6 x 6 vehicle, where there are two axles at the rear of the vehicle to support the weight on the rear, this two-axle combination is the "rear bogie." An 8 x 8 vehicle with two axles on each end would have a "front bogie" and a "rear bogie."

18. Center of Gravity. The point within a vehicle at which all of its weight may be considered to be concentrated. When a vehicle is tipped to a degree that a vertical line passing through the center of gravity falls on the ground outside the axle tread track, it is unstable and will turn over easily.

19. Chassis. The assembled frame, engine, drive train, and tires of a vehicle.

20. Clean Agent. An electrically nonconducting volatile or gaseous fire extinguishing agent that does not leave a residue upon evaporation and has shown to provide extinguishing action equivalent to halon 2111 under the test protocol of FAA Technical Report DOT/FAA/AR-95/87.

21. Combined Agent Vehicle. An ARFF vehicle that carries water/foam as the primary extinguishing agent and either a dry chemical, Clean Agent, or approved equivalent, or another acceptable agent as the complementary agent. A "dual-agent" vehicle is one designed so that the turret and/or handline can separately or simultaneously discharge both primary and complementary agents.

22. Component Manufacturer's Certification. A signed application approval furnished by the manufacturer certifying that the component in question is acceptable as being—

    a. Properly installed.

    b. Suitable for service as applied in the vehicle for its intended use.

    c. In compliance with the respective construction criteria required by this AC.

23. Coolant Preheater Device. A device for heating the engine coolant so the engine maintains a constant temperature. It usually consists of a coolant jacket and an electric heating element. The engine coolant flows through the preheater jacket and absorbs heat from a heating element. The heating element obtains its power from an outside source, thereby holding the engine coolant at a temperature recommended for fast starting.

24. Critical Rescue and Fire Fighting Access Area (CRFFAA). The rectangular area on an airport surrounding any runway within which historical data has shown that most aircraft accidents can be expected to occur. NFPA describes it as an area included by a rectangle that extends in width 500 feet (150 m) on each side of the centerline of the runway times a length that includes the runway plus 3,300 feet (1,000 m) beyond each end of the runway.

Area in ft^2 = 1,000 ft x [runway length(ft) + 6,600 ft] or

Area in m^2 = 300 m x [runway length(m) + 2,000 m]

25. Dual Agent Nozzle or Turret. A fire fighting appliance designed to dispense foam and a complementary agent, individually or simultaneously.

26. Eductor. A device designed to proportion liquid foam concentrate into a water/foam system. The device may be part of a vehicle foam agent system or it may be portable.

27. Film-Forming Foam. A foam liquid concentrate, when mixed in appropriate proportions with water and applied to the surface of a flammable liquid, forms a film on the surface of the fuel that suppresses vaporization with or without the presence of visible foam.

28. Fluid Coupling. A turbine-like device that transmits power solely through the action of a fluid in a closed circuit (i.e., no direct mechanical connection between input and output shafts) and without torque multiplication.

29. Fluoroprotein Foam Concentrate. A protein foam concentrate incorporating one or more fluorochemical surfactants to enhance its tolerance to fuel contamination.

30. Foam Expansion Ratio. The number used to express the relationship between the volume of foam produced and the volume of water/foam solution used in its production.

31. Foam Liquid Concentrate Percentage. The numerical designation of the amount of foam-liquid concentrate in solution with water.

32. Fully Loaded Vehicle. The fully assembled vehicle, complete with a complement of crew, fuel, equipment, and fire fighting agents. The crew allowance shall be 225 pounds (102 kg) per seating position. The equipment allowance for performance tests is a maximum of 1,000 pounds (450 kg) or the actual weight of the equipment provided by the vehicle manufacturer, whichever is higher.

33. In-Service Condition. A state or condition of readiness for intended duty. Usually an emergency vehicle properly serviced with all equipment properly loaded and ready for immediate response; i.e., a fully loaded vehicle.

34. Interaxle Clearance Angle (Ramp Angle). Describes the sharpest "height of land" over which a vehicle can pass without hanging up. Clearance is determined by the angles formed by the horizontal ground line between the closest forward and rear axles and whichever of the following lines form the smallest angle:

    a. The line tangent to the loaded radius of the front tire, extended rearward to that fixed point on the vehicle ahead of a vertical line midway between the two axles, that will determine the smallest angle.

    b. The line tangent to the loaded radius of the rear tire, extended forward to that fixed point on the vehicle behind a vertical line midway between the two axles, that will determine the smallest angle.

35. Interaxle Differential. A differential in the line of drive between any two axles.

36. Lightweight Construction. Intended to indicate the use of nonferrous metals, composites, or plastics or a reduction in weight by the use of advanced engineering practices, resulting in a weight saving without sacrificing strength, durability, or efficiency.

37. Listed. Equipment or materials included in a list published by an organization (acceptable to the authority having jurisdiction) concerned with product evaluation. The organization performs periodic inspection of production items of the listed equipment or materials. Its listing states either that the equipment or materials meets appropriate standards or passes tests and, therefore, has been found suitable for use in a specified manner.

38. May. This term states a permissive use or an alternative method to meet a specified requirement. It is intended to describe an option available to the manufacturer, unless otherwise noted.

39. No-Load Condition. An engine with standard accessories operating without an imposed load with the vehicle drive clutches and any special accessory clutches in a disengaged or neutral condition.

40. Off-Pavement Performance. This refers to a vehicle's ability to perform or operate on other than paved surfaces. These "other than paved surfaces" include dirt roads, trails, and a wide variety of open cross-country terrain. Other references to this capability may be in terms of "off-road mobility" or "cross-country mobility." These three terms are synonymous.

41. Overall Height, Length, and Width. The dimensions determined with the vehicle fully loaded and equipped. Unless otherwise specified, the measurements shall include all protrusions that could in any way hinder the passage of the vehicle. Dimensions determined for movable protrusions shall be with the protrusion in its normally stowed position.

42. Percent Grade. The ratio of the change in elevation (rise) to the horizontal distance (run) traveled multiplied by 100. Example: A change in elevation of 50 feet (15 m) over a horizontal distance of 50 feet (15 m) is a 100-percent grade. This is also known as a 45-degree angle or 1:1 slope.

43. Power-Assisted Steering. A system using hydraulic or air power to aid in the steering. This system is supplementary to the mechanical system required to preserve steering ability in event of power failure.

44. Protein Foam Concentrate. A concentrated solution of hydrolyzed protein plus stabilizing additives and inhibitors to protect against freezing, prevent corrosion of equipment and containers, resist bacterial decomposition, control viscosity, and otherwise assure readiness for use.

45. Prototype Vehicle. The first of a unique vehicle configuration built to establish the performance capability not only of itself, but of all subsequent vehicles manufactured from the same basic drawings and parts list. A given chassis, body, fire fighting system, and fully loaded weight condition shall constitute a vehicle configuration. Product improvements and/or customer options shall negate a given, previously conducted, prototype test only if the changes can be reasonably expected to materially affect the given performance factor.

46. Radio Interference Suppression. Suppression of the ignition and electrical system noises that normally interfere with radio transmission and reception.

47. Rubber-Gasketed Fitting. A device for providing a leak-proof connection between two pieces of pipe while allowing moderate movement of one pipe relative to the other. It incorporates a rubber seal held in place by a two-piece clamp that also engages annular grooves near the end of each pipe to prevent pullout under pressure.

48. Shall. Indicates a mandatory requirement. It is applicable to vehicles purchased using Federal funding.

49. Should. This term indicates a recommendation or advice but not a requirement.

50. Steering Drive Ends. The ends/stub shafts in the wheel spindle in a driving-steering axle used on the steering axle(s) of an all-wheel drive ARFF vehicle.

51. Torque Converter. A device similar to the fluid coupling but that, by means of additional turbine blades, results in torque multiplication.

52. Ton. The equivalent of 2,000 U.S. pounds (907 kg).

53. Twenty-Five-Percent Drainage Time. The time, in minutes, that it takes for 25 percent of the total liquid contained in a known volume of foam to drain out. It is one means of evaluating the performance of foam producing devices. NFPA 412 gives a method of measuring drainage time.

54. Underbody or Underchassis Clearance. The minimum dimension between the ground and any components of the vehicle, except those that are part of the axle assemblies, that could hinder the passage of the vehicle. This dimension is determined with the vehicle fully loaded and fully equipped, unless otherwise specified.

55. Unitized Rigid Body and Frame Structure. A form of vehicle construction that integrates parts (generally comprising a separate body) with the chassis frame to form one rigid, load-carrying structure.

56. Unsprung Weight. The total weight of all vehicle components that are not completely supported by the suspension system.

57. Vehicle Drive Nomenclature. Common vehicle references are 4 x 2, 4 x 4, 6 x 6, and 8 x 8. In the use of this nomenclature, the first number indicates the total number of wheels on the vehicle and the second number is the number of driving wheels.

58. Wall-to-Wall Turning Diameter. The smallest diameter circle described by the outermost point on the vehicle as it negotiates a 360-degree right or left turn.

59. Weathertight. Compartment closure sufficient to prevent rain, snow, wind-driven sand, dirt, or dust from penetrating under most operating conditions. It is not necessary to be watertight, vaportight, dustproof, or submersible.

60. Weight Scale Measurement. The accurate measurement of vehicle weight by means of a scale to verify or check a stated or estimated weight.

APPENDIX 2. OFF-PAVEMENT MOBILITY.

Section 1. Background.

1. There have been many attempts by individuals and institutions to identify the controlling parameters in the design of ARFF vehicles suitable for both paved and off-pavement service. While this capability is evasive, easily misunderstood, and expensive to achieve, it is a necessary one.

2. A review of the available aircraft accident statistics should convince even most skeptics of the need for good off-pavement performance. For example, when past accident locations are mapped, as shown in Figure A-2.1, you can clearly see that a large percentage of the aircraft accidents occur off runways and other paved surfaces. Hence, to be truly effective, ARFF vehicles require certain off-pavement mobility capabilities while retaining general highway performance requirements.

3. In addition, Figure A-2.1 supports the premise that the highest potential benefit in terms of reducing future aircraft accident deaths by fire can be obtained by achieving the capability to perform the ARFF service life safety mission in the off-pavement environment of the airport. This capability is most effectively achieved through two complementary efforts.

4. First, survey the airport in question to identify those areas that lie within the airport's Critical Rescue and Fire Fighting Access Area (CRFFAA) that cannot be traversed by the existing fleet of straight-framed, wheeled vehicles. If the size and/or distribution of these nontraversable areas is small relative to the CRFFAA, preplan alternate access routes (permanent or seasonal, as appropriate) to potential accident sites, and train the vehicle operators to avoid the use of these nontraversable areas during an emergency response. The objective of providing such a training program for the designated ARFF vehicle operators is to ensure that they are familiar with the preferred alternate routes to likely accident sites, have knowledge of the operational limitations of their specific vehicles, and have the opportunity to practice their off-pavement driving skills over the designated alternate routes.

5. If the action taken above still leaves the airport with relatively large sections of difficult terrain (e.g., low soil strength, grades over 10 percent, rocky areas, swamp lands, deep snow, or bodies of water) that lie inside the airport's CRFFAA, the ARFF system manager should consider the specification of an ARFF service vehicle other than the ordinary straight-frame, wheeled ARFF vehicles. Examples of such vehicles are straight-frame tracked; articulating, wheeled, or tracked; amphibious; air cushioned; or a combination of these types.

6. The off-pavement performance characteristics of any ground-supported vehicle depend on numerous factors. Although considerable progress has been made in the continuing effort to identify these factors and to design for the controlling parameters of off-pavement vehicle performance, there are still many left with which to deal. Nevertheless, the following factors, while not all inclusive, have been identified as important considerations in specifying a vehicle for off-pavement ARFF operations. Primary among those factors identified are the capabilities of the driver; topography of the area and soil trafficability; the vehicle's total geometric, inertial, and mechanical characteristics; and tire selection.

7. An ARFF vehicle with special mobility requirements or the adaption of a unique vehicle for ARFF service is expensive. Therefore, any special vehicle performance criteria identified as a result of an assessment of the airport's off-pavement mobility requirements must be addressed in quantitative terms to the maximum extent possible. In other words, the purchaser should make it perfectly clear what the ARFF vehicle manufacturer is being asked to provide before the bids are opened.

8. THROUGH 19. RESERVED.

Section 2. Tire Selection.

20. Tire diameter, width, inflation pressure, and deflection (as related to the loads imposed) are important basic elements. The use of treads designed to provide traction, skid resistance, and self-cleaning is a good consideration.

21. To optimize vehicle performance characteristics (i.e., achieve the best combination of acceleration, speed, braking, and maneuvering capabilities for both on and off-pavement), both the vehicle and the tire manufacturers must have accurate information about the intended service environment.

22. When local conditions require high floatation (sand, mud, snow, etc.) and good traction for off-pavement mobility, vehicle tires shall have a tread suitable to develop a drawbar pull of 0.4 times the vehicle weight on a level, clean, clay surface [CL in Unified Soil Classification System (USCS)], with a strength of 200 or greater Rating Cone Index (RCI)

immediately after a half inch per hour rainfall intensity storm.

23. Low-inflation pressures that improve off-road mobility also increase the likelihood of hydroplaning on flooded pavements. The central tire inflation option may be specified on vehicles to be used both on- and off-road.

24. THROUGH 29. RESERVED.

Section 3. General Topography and Soil Trafficability.

30. The U.S. Army Corps of Engineers at the Waterways Experiment Station at Vicksburg, MS, has, over a period of 30 years of testing, developed an approach to this multifaceted parameter that they call the vehicle cone index (VCI). The VCI is a method of estimating the probability of a vehicle of given characteristics successfully operating in a given off-pavement soil condition. Although not accepted by some ARFF vehicle manufacturers, the concept is certainly noteworthy.

31. Furthermore, it is strongly recommended that those planning to develop a specification for an ARFF vehicle pay particular attention to the uniqueness of the entire off-pavement environment at their specific airports. As discussed earlier, special attention should be given to the unpaved surfaces inside the CRFFAA. If there is any doubt about accident site accessibility due to questionable soil trafficability, a soil strength survey should be performed to determine the VCI of proposed access routes. The survey should be conducted during the time of year when the strength of the soil involved is at its poorest. This additional effort could pay big dividends in terms of cost-effectiveness.

32. The VCI is a means of determining vehicle weight bearing requirements compared to soil strength (cone index) in a particular situation. The calculated VCI number for the vehicle should be less than the measured soil strength in a particular situation to assure successful operation. Vehicles operating on different types of soil will exhibit different levels of traction performance. Therefore, separate computations are required to predict soil-vehicle performance for fine-grained and coarse-grained soils.

33. In general, the vehicle having the lowest VCI will have the highest probability of negotiating a given off-pavement condition. If, as a result of a soil strength survey, the purchaser must clearly specify the VCI is going to be used as a selection criteria as a performance requirement item in the request for bids, the manufacturers should provide the VCI for their specific vehicle designs as part of their bid responses.

34. THROUGH 39. RESERVED.

Section 4. Geometric, Inertial, and Mechanical Characteristics.

40. The full acceleration and top speed characteristics of the vehicle required in Chapter 2, Section 7, and Table 2 are not, in and of themselves, very useful in the off-pavement environment. However, the power required to produce that performance has a second, equally important function. In a well-designed vehicle, the same power needed to meet the acceleration and top speed requirements can also be used to maneuver in the

off-pavement environment. The requirement for that power has been quantified in Paragraph 55, Gradability.

41. The same vehicle design features that, in the aggregate, produce unstable performance in the operational environment on paved surfaces are magnified in the off-pavement situation. Hence, it must be emphasized that stability is essential in any ARFF vehicle. These characteristics have been quantified in terms of both static and dynamic stability in Paragraph 53.

42. It is also important that a vehicle intended for off-pavement service be designed to minimize the potential for getting hung up on obstacles commonly encountered in the intended operational environment. Although universal agreement may never be reached, a significant degree of standardization has been attained. Items of particular concern are angles of approach, departure, and interaxle clearance; underbody and underaxle clearances; and wall-to-wall turning diameter. Quantified requirements for these items can be found in Table 2.

43. Specifying unique values for other physical, non-performance related features—such as overall height, width, length, exact turning radius, or gross vehicle weight—becomes very complex and, with very few exceptions, contributes nothing to the enhancement of the vehicle's off-pavement mobility performance capability. In general, these features are payload dependent. Put another way, before these dimensions/clearances can be optimized, the specific payload characteristics must be identified. As the independent variable, payload tends to dictate the practical range within which such features can be specified. In addition, the final result is usually the byproduct of a specific manufacturer's overall design approach and as a result, is often proprietary in nature.

44. THROUGH 49. RESERVED

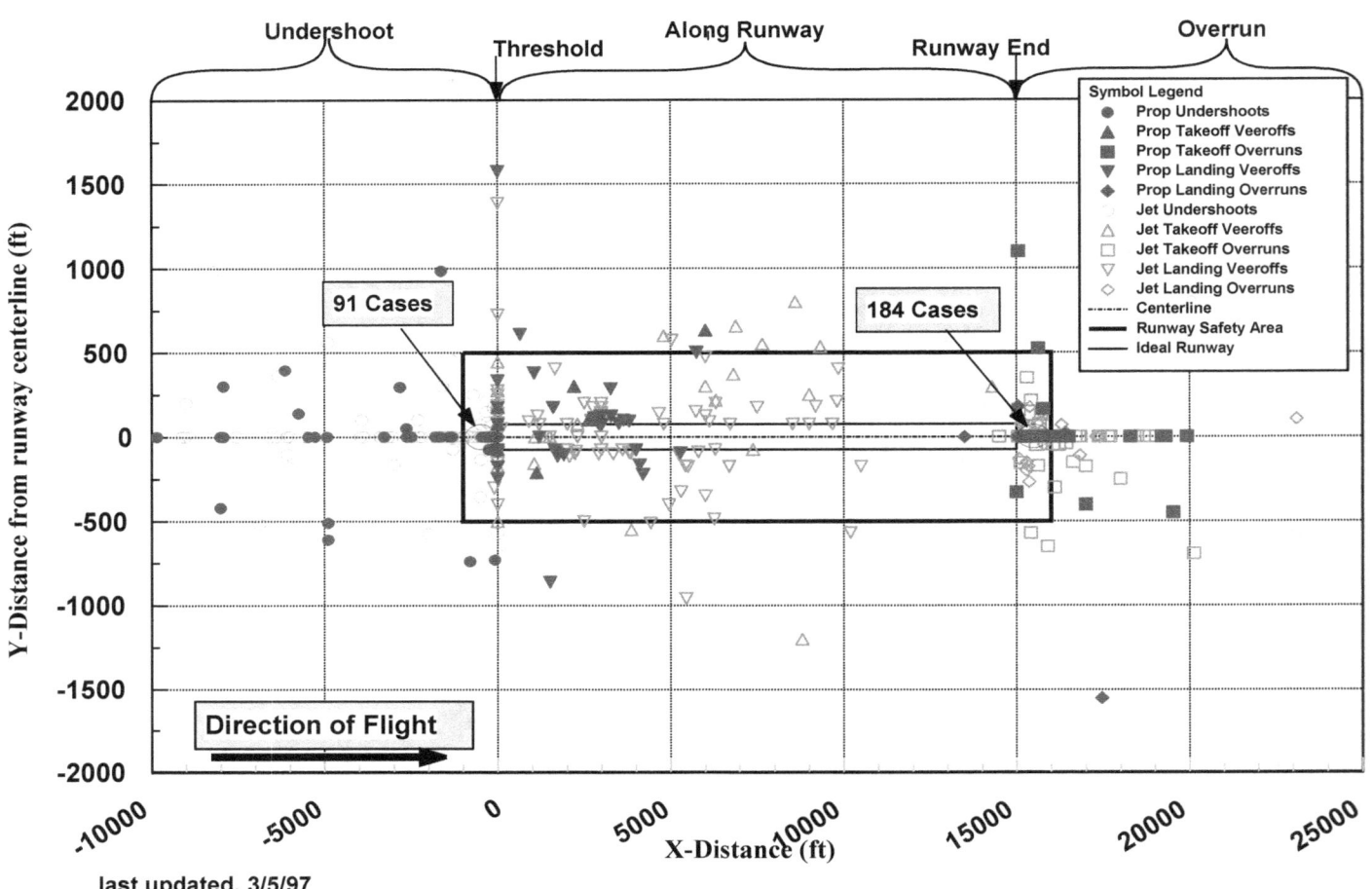

Figure A-2.1. Location of Landing and Takeoff Accidents (Source: ALPA)

APPENDIX 3. EQUIPMENT FOR
AIRCRAFT RESCUE AND FIRE FIGHTING OPERATIONS.

Section 1. General-Use Equipment and Tools and Personnel Protective Equipment.

1. A list of recommended equipment and tools is given in table A-3.1. The range of equipment is broken out by both certificated airport ARFF Index and general aviation airports.

Table A-3.1. Recommended Equipment for Rescue Operations (Page 1).

AUXILIARY EQUIPMENT, INCLUDING	AIRPORT ARFF INDEX OR CATEGORY			
	GA-1	GA-2 & A	B-C	D-E
Axe, rescue, large, non-wedge type with serrated edge and 36-inch (91.4 cm) fiberglass handle; to include scabbard and pick head cover	1	1	2	2
Blanket, fire resistant with storage pouch	1	1	2	2
Chock, aluminum, 8 inch (20.3 cm)	2	2	2	2
Cutter, bolt, 24 inch (61cm)	1	1	1	1
Cutter, cable, aircraft	1	1	1	1
Prybar, 60 inch (152.4 cm)	1	1	1	1
Hammer, sledge, 8 pound (3.6 kg)	1	1	1	1
Hook, assault grapnel, 3 hooks, 2 pound (.9 kg)	1	1	1	1
Ladder, extension or "A-Frame", minimum 20-foot (6.1 m) overall length	1	1	1	1
Lantern, rechargeable–installed in cab (12 or 24 volt, as applicable)	*	*	*	*
Medical kit, first aid/first responder trauma kit, 76 component minimum w/ nylon tote bag	1	1	1	1
Pike pole, 8 foot (3.6 m) with fiberglass handle	1	1	1	1
Rescue kit, hydraulic, 10 ton (manual type without auxiliary power source)	1	1	1	1
Rescue kit, pneumatic air hammer standard duty type), complete with spare air cylinder	1	1	1	1
Saw, powered rescue, 14 inch (35.6 cm), complete with two (2) spare blades	1	1	1	1
Skin penetrator (piercing applicator), for water or foam application, manual type	1	1	1	1
OR				
Skin penetrator, for water, foam, or dry chemical application, pneumatic type, including carrying case, adaptor, and compressed air cylinder	1	1	1	1
Wrench, adjustable, 8 inch (20.3 cm)	1	1	1	1

* One for each seating position on vehicle.

Table A-3.1. Recommended Equipment for Rescue Operations (Page 2).

FORCIBLE ENTRY TOOL KIT INCLUDING	AIRPORT ARFF INDEX OR CATEGORY			
	GA-1	GA-2 & A	B-C	D-E
Axe, rescue, small, non-wedge type with serrated edge, sheath and insulated handle	1	2	3	3
Chisel, cold, 1 inch (2.5 cm)	1	1	1	1
Hacksaw, heavy duty, 12 inch (30.5 cm) with pistol grip and six (6) assorted blades	1	1	1	1
Hammer, 1-1/4 pound (.6 kg)	1	1	1	1
Hammer, 4 pound (1.8 kg)	1	1	1	1
Knife, rescue, V-blade (harness cutting tool)	1	1	3	3
Pliers, side cutting, 7 inch (17.8 cm)	1	1	1	1
Plug, fuel line (hardwood)	3	3	3	3
Plug, fuel line (neoprene)	3	3	3	3
Rope line, nylon, 100 foot (30 m), 5/8 inch (16 mm)	1	1	1	1
Screwdriver set–three (3) Phillips and three (3) straight blade	1	1	1	1
Shears, sheet metal, straight cut	1	1	1	1
Wrecking bar (crowbar), 36 inch (91.4 cm)	1	1	1	1
Wrench, vice grip, 10 inch (24.5 cm)	1	1	1	1

This Page Intentionally Left Blank

APPENDIX 4. PURCHASER ELECTION OF SUBSYSTEM COMPONENTS.

Section 1. Background.

1. The Federal Aviation Administration (FAA), airport sponsors, and manufacturers of airport rescue and fire fighting (ARFF) vehicles, working together, created this ARFF vehicle specification based on quantitative and verifiable performance criteria.

2. This guide specification is intended to permit manufacturers to bid competitively and to preclude the need for the purchaser to be involved in materials selection. It does, however, provide the purchaser a menu of subsystem options related to local operational criteria and vehicle cost-effectiveness. Thus, it gives the purchaser the opportunity to make the purchased vehicle "fit" the airport's identifiable operational needs while avoiding the continuous string of time-consuming protests triggered by the proprietary or exclusionary nature of the request for bids that favor a manufacturer.

3. It should be noted that the prospective bidder should determine the means to be used to fulfill all of the remaining automotive and fire extinguishing subsystem performance criteria not included in that menu.

4. THROUGH 19. RESERVED.

Section 2. Option Selection Worksheets.

20. This guide specification provides numerous opportunities for the purchaser to make subsystem component/performance selections that affect the vehicle characteristics. A paragraph-by-paragraph list (menu) of those vehicle characteristics that are specifically reserved for the purchaser has been assembled in the form of a selection worksheet. A checklist is provided in the right-hand column of the worksheet on which the purchaser may indicate which of the available options are required to tailor the vehicle to the needs of his/her specific airport.

21. If a purchaser believes that additional items or modifications (including the selection of the means to fulfill the required performance now reserved for prospective bidders) are needed to fulfill local, **identifiable operational requirements**, they should be added below this basic list. These additional modifications must be accompanied by a detailed, rational justification for departing from the performance-oriented nature of the guide specification. For Federally funded procurements, this justification must be approved by the FAA.

22. The contractor will supply a water/foam aircraft rescue and fire fighting vehicle meeting the requirements of FAA AC 150/5220-10C, Guide Specification for Water/Foam Aircraft Rescue and Fire Fighting Vehicles, dated 2/18/02, subject to the attached clarifications. The clarifications listed are the ONLY differences from the minimum standard vehicle meeting the requirements of the AC.

Table A-4.1. Worksheet for Subsystem Component Selection.

A. The following clarifications are specifically noted in the AC as purchaser options and require no further justification.

(Name and Title of FAA Approving Official)

WORKSHEET FOR SUBSYSTEM COMPONENT SELECTION			
AC Para. Number:	Paragraph Title or Subsystem Description:	Rationale for Position:	Purchaser's Selection:
Chapter 1. Introduction			
5.a	Seat belts: Shoulder Harness Systems		3-points restraint seat belts: For driver only: For all positions:
5.e	Provisions for mounting radios	The specific provisions for mounting radios are a function of the type, size, shape, and operational configuration of the radio in service at the airport or being ordered as part of the vehicle purchase. Therefore, it must be tailored to the individual airport's requirements. The radio and the mounting are not a vehicle performance item.	Type and location of radio:
11.k	Installation of continuous ..... extend useful life of the vehicle	Continuous duty cycle lubrication systems for suspension parts have shown the ability to extend the time before repair and costly maintenance is required on over-the-road as well as heavy excavation equipment. The installation of this type of system is in line with the FAA's goal of extending vehicle service life	Yes_____ No _____
13.	Requirement to comply with painting and marking standard... AC 150/5210-5B	AC 150/5210-5B, Painting, Marking, and Lighting of Vehicles Used On an Airport, Paragraph 7.b, provides for customizing the vehicle paint scheme in terms of vehicle number, airport name, reflective striping, and the airport's insignia. The original application of decorative paint schemes is expensive. The retrofitting of these paint schemes is prohibitively expensive. Therefore, detailed requirements for each of these items should be clearly defined before requesting bids on the vehicle.	Numbers: Side: Size _____ Roof: Size _____ Reflective striping: Yes_____ No_____ Airport name: Yes _____ No _____ Airport logo: Yes _____No _____

WORKSHEET FOR SUBSYSTEM COMPONENT SELECTION

AC Para. Number:	Paragraph Title or Subsystem Description:	Rationale for Position:	Purchaser's Selection:
14.	Insulation, Waterproofing, Air Conditioning, and Winterization	The need for AC and winterization are subject to climatic, geographical, and operational considerations that are airport specific.	Air conditioning required: Yes ——— No ——— Winterization required: Yes ——— No———
Chapter 2. Automotive System			
26.c	The election of a "pintle hook" in addition to "two towing eyes…"	Towing other vehicles with an ARFF vehicle is not a common practice. However, some operators believe that the pintle hook enhances operational flexibility. The substitution of it for the two rear-towing hooks/eyes, that are intended to facilitate ARFF vehicle recovery in the case of breakdown or a stuck vehicle, does not impact the vehicle's fire fighting performance or, to any great extent, its recoverability.	Pintle hook: Yes ——— No ———
27.	AC Control Windshield Deluge System Control	See Item #14. See Item #29.	AC control: Yes _____ No _____ Windshield deluge system control: Yes _____ No _____
28.f	Heated Mirrors	The heated mirrors might be helpful to the driver/crew member to see clearly in the bad weather.	Heated mirrors: Yes _____ No _____
29.	Equipment	In addition to the function of the windshield washers and wipers, a system to flush the windshield may be advantageous on vehicles with roof mounted turrets.	Windshield deluge system: Yes _____ No _____ Air conditioner: Yes: _____ No: _____ Backup monitor: Yes: _____ No: _____

WORKSHEET FOR SUBSYSTEM COMPONENT SELECTION			
AC Para. Number:	Paragraph Title or Subsystem Description:	Rationale for Position:	Purchaser's Selection:
32.a.(3) and 32.a.(4)	Means to keep brake system air reservoir up to operational pressure...	The vehicle brake air system performance requirement is specified. Which of the two and recognized methods used to keep the vehicle brake air pressure operational does not impact the "as-built" vehicle performance. However, it may impact its cost-effectiveness if the method used is not compatible with local resources. Hence, it is viewed as a local operational decision.	110V or 220V auxiliary onboard compressor: _____ OR House air fitting: _____
37.g	Beadlocks	If tires will be operated at low pressure, beadlocks may be desirable.	Provide beadlocks: Yes _____ No _____
39.c	Optional lighting items...	These lighting items do not affect the fire fighting performance of the vehicle and are not wanted by some operators. Hence, they are not required for vehicle approval. Conversely, other operators identify various lighting items as an operational requirement. This is particularly true at airports where there is no other source for auxiliary onsite lighting. Hence, a variety of lighting items are retained as optional accessories that purchasers may request on an "as needed" basis.	Identify and list items being selected: Fog light(s): Yes _____ No _____ Spotlight(s): Yes _____ No _____ Quartz Light(s): Yes _____ No _____ Amber flashing beacon: Yes _____ No _____
40.d.(1), (2), and (3)	Mounting Location and Type for Shore Power Plugs	The mounting location does not affect the vehicle performance. The local firehouse wiring configuration or personnel traffic patterns will dictate the most cost-effective or operationally advantageous location.	Identify & specify required location and specify components to be connected.
43.a	Radio Equipment	The radio equipment may include boom/microphone headsets with appropriate controls, radio interconnects, and remote or foot-operated push-to-talk switches, as specified by the purchaser. If a vehicle is to be equipped with headsets, storage boxes shall be provided to protect this equipment.	Headsets: Yes _____ No _____

		WORKSHEET FOR SUBSYSTEM COMPONENT SELECTION	
AC Para. Number:	Paragraph Title or Subsystem Description:	Rationale for Position:	Purchaser's Selection:
45.b	Exhaust System	A curved exhaust stack or a straight exhaust pipe with rain cap shall be provided as specified.	Curved exhaust stack: _____ Or Straight exhaust pipe: _____
46.e	Heated Fuel Water Separator	A fuel water separator shall be provided; however, not all geographical areas require heated.	Heated fuel water separator required: Yes _____ No _____
50.	Winterization	See Item #14.	
Chapter 3. Fire Extinguishing Systems			
Section 1	Dry Chemical–Sodium or Potassium Bicarbonate Based **or** Section 2. Clean Agent or an acceptable substitute– Option or an acceptable substitute	The inclusion of a complementary agent system option as part of a major ARFF vehicle is intended to facilitate the purchaser's selection of the ARFF vehicle fleet configuration that best fits the local operational situation and still complies with 14 CFR Part 139. It should be noted that in addition to 14 CFR Part139 requirements, fire service managers must consider their obligations under the Montreal Protocol Treaty regarding the limited (essential) use of Clean Agent or approved equivalent as a fire fighting agent.	Dry chemical required: Yes _____ No _____ Clean Agent or approved equivalent or substitute required: Yes _____ No _____
72.f	Hoisting System	Aid in propellant cylinder change.	Lift system required: Manual: _____ Electric: _____
73.a.(1)	Clean Agent or Approved Equivalent Agent Container	The option to select less than the normal 500-pound (225 kg) container is in recognition of the airport fire service's obligations under the Montreal Protocol to select and use Clean Agent or approved equivalent **only** where no other agent will perform the task.	Identify agent: _____ Specify container capacity in pounds: _____
76.a.(1) and 76.a.(2)	Concentrate Proportioner ...range of accuracy...	For a given foam type, the fire extinguishing performance of the water/foam solutions for 6% and 3% foam concentrates is the same. However, cost-effectiveness and/or operational compatibility with mutual aid resupply sources may dictate the need for one or the other. Proportioner performance is sensitive to both foam	Agent concentrate to be used in vehicle: 6% _____ OR 3% _____

	WORKSHEET FOR SUBSYSTEM COMPONENT SELECTION		
AC Para. Number:	Paragraph Title or Subsystem Description:	Rationale for Position:	Purchaser's Selection:
		type and the concentration. Therefore, purchasers must identify which foam type and which foam concentrate (not the proportioner) is to be used.	
78.b.	EXCEPTION: Adapters, ...	There is a national standard for fire hose and hose connections. However, not all jurisdictions have completed the transition. Hence, to ensure that the vehicle is compatible with local fittings and that effective mutual aid arrangements can be achieved, adapters for nonstandard fittings may be specified.	Adapters required: Yes _____ No _____ Identify specific type.
78.k	Limited Structural Exterior Panel	A limited structural exterior panel can be specified by the purchaser as listed in 78.k.	Yes: _____ No: _____
78.l	Priming Pump and Reservoir		Yes: _____ No: _____
80.a.(2)	Water Reservoir and Piping... materials compatibility with local water characteristics.	This provision is not intended to involve the purchaser in the selection of materials. It is, however, intended to minimize the lifetime costs of vehicle ownership by alerting both the manufacturer and the purchaser of the need to identify the most likely sources of water to be used in the ARFF vehicle and to ensure that the properties of that water and the materials selected by the manufacturer for tank fabrication and the related piping are compatible.	Airport ARFF water supply has unusual characteristics: Yes _____ No _____ Identify unusual properties:
80.a(8)	Thread Connection	The purchaser shall specify the size and type of thread connection.	Thread connection: Size: Type:
81.a.	Twinned or Separate Water/Foam and Complementary Agent Handlines	The method of mounting the handline does not affect the fire extinguishing performance. However, depending on the complementary agent chosen and/or the operational tactics used at a specific airport, one method may be more cost-effective than the other. Recent USAF/FAA large fire research has shown that nozzles that entrain or capture dry chemical into the agent master stream provide significant improvements in fighting three	Separate agent handlines: _____ OR Twinned agent handlines: _____

		WORKSHEET FOR SUBSYSTEM COMPONENT SELECTION		
AC Para. Number:	Paragraph Title or Subsystem Description:	Rationale for Position:	Purchaser's Selection:	
		dimensional running fuel fires, a common fire scenario encountered.		
81.b. and 81.c.	Reeled Handlines or Woven, Multiple Jacket Handlines	The inclusion of both types of handlines is intended to provide the purchaser a choice that will be compatible with the airport fire department's operational requirements.	Reeled, hard rubber handline: OR Woven jacket handlines in hose bed:	
83.a.(5)	Be fitted with...	USAF/FAA large fire research has shown that nozzles that entrain or capture dry chemical into the agent master stream provide significant improvements in fighting three dimensional running fuel fires, a common fire scenario encountered.	Dry chemical discharge from the primary turret: Yes _____ No _____	
84.e	Secondary Turret	This choice between automatic oscillation controls is permitted to allow for differences in operation tactic.	Control with: Fixed oscillation angle of 90° each side of the center: _____ Total traverse of at least 180° increment adjustable oscillation angles: _____	
87	Dual Agent Turret	The dual agent turret shall meet the requirements in paragraph 87.	Dual agent turret: Yes: _____ No: _____	
89	Complementary Agent System	A dry chemical or clean agent system can be specified by the purchaser but it shall meet the requirements set forth in Table 3 or Table 3M	Dry chemical system: Yes: _____ No: _____ Clean agent system: Yes: _____ No: _____	
Table A-3.1	Skin Penetrator (Piercing Applicator)	The purchaser may specify the type of skin penetrator (piercing penetrator) for water, foam, or dry chemical application.	Skin penetrator type: Manual: _____ Pneumatic: _____	

This Page Intentionally Left Blank

B. The following clarifications are specifically noted in the AC as purchaser options that require approval by the local FAA Airports District or Regional Office. They are approved as noted below:

_____

(Name and Title of FAA Approving Official)

WORKSHEET FOR SUBSYSTEM COMPONENT SELECTION			
AC Para. Number:	Paragraph Title or Subsystem Description:	Rationale for Position:	Purchaser's Selection:
21.	Dimensions	In the case of overall vehicle dimensions, there is the potential conflict between the vehicle size in one or more of its dimensions with the local operating environment. If not provided for, this could reduce the overall cost-effectiveness of the performance-based specification by either restricting operational flexibility or by requiring expensive facility modifications. A justification is required for each specific dimension that is requested.	Required specific dimensions: Length: _____ Height: _____ Width: _____ Justification:
28.a.(1)	More than two crew positions...	The need for a seating configuration to accommodate more than two ARFF personnel per vehicle is a function of local operational practices. Therefore, it is included as an option available to the purchaser.	Number of seats: _____ Justification:
58.b	Central Tire Inflation/ Deflation System	The central inflation/deflation system may enhance the traction capability of the vehicle in certain terrain. The automatic preset pressure for the system would also allow the airport to customize this feature to their particular terrain and allow the operator to quickly set up the vehicle for a seamless move from paved to unpaved conditions.	Justification for central inflation/deflation system:

WORKSHEET FOR SUBSYSTEM COMPONENT SELECTION

AC Para. Number:	Paragraph Title or Subsystem Description:	Rationale for Position:	Purchaser's Selection:
59.b & c	DEVS	The DEVS equipment can aid normal operations, improve emergency response time, and provide an additional margin of safety for airport rescue response during very low-visibility operations. FLIR camera of DEVS is required; however, the navigation and/or tracking subsystem is optional, and justifications are needed.	Justification for: Navigation subsystem: Tracking subsystem:
79.c(4)	Water pump	Water pump shall be constructed of materials that are compatible with water, water/foam solutions, and foam concentrate. However, a bronze water pump shall be supplied should local water conditions require additional protection from corrosive, acidic, or salt water conditions.	Justification:
83.a(6)	Primary Turret	The primary turret will be operated with power-assist; otherwise, justification is needed.	Justification:
85.	High-Reach Extendable Turret- Option	A USAF/FAA-sponsored large fire research has shown significant fire knockdown improvements with ground-level or low-ground positioning (close to the fuel surface and parallel to ground agent applications) of AFFF. In large pool fire tests, increased efficiency resulted with extremely rapid pool fire control or knockdown. The election of a high-reach extendable turret option will improve agent application techniques over standard roof turret designs. Testing has also verified rapid interior cooling and expulsion of smoke and toxic gasses when a boom-mounted piercing applicator is used to penetrate the fuselage. This rapid improvement of interior conditions provides a safer environment for firefighters to enter for rescue and final extinguishment.	High-Reach Extendable Turret: Yes _____ No _____ Justification:

WORKSHEET FOR SUBSYSTEM COMPONENT SELECTION			
AC Para. Number:	Paragraph Title or Subsystem Description:	Rationale for Position:	Purchaser's Selection:
86	Man-rated Aerials.	There should be a distinction made between a man-rated aerial device and a high-reach extendible turret. Each is a valuable tool; however, there are significant differences in their capabilities and restrictions. Each airport can find special benefits by operating a man-rated aerial in their ARFF fleet.	Man-rated Aerials: Yes _____ No _____ Justification:
88.	Undertruck Nozzles – Option	One of the purposes of the undertruck nozzles is to protect the vehicle and crew in the event of sudden fire under the apparatus.	Undertruck nozzles: Yes _____ No _____ Justification:

This Page Intentionally Left Blank

C.   The following clarifications are not specifically noted in the AC as purchaser options. For Federally funded procurements, they may only be approved through the issuance of a Modification to Standards by the local FAA Airports District or Regional Office. The Modification to Standards has been issued as noted below.

_____

(Name and Title of FAA Approving Official)

(Sponsor to attach list of modifications to be requested through the Modification to Standards process.)

End Page Intentionally Left Blank

www.ingramcontent.com/pod-product-compliance
Lightning Source LLC
Chambersburg PA
CBHW081118290526
45795CB00006B/2162

* 9 7 8 1 4 9 4 2 6 0 5 0 7 *